Lobster

Animal
Series editor: Jonathan Burt

Lobster

Richard J. King

REAKTION BOOKS

Published by
REAKTION BOOKS LTD
33 Great Sutton Street
London EC1V 0DX, UK
www.reaktionbooks.co.uk

First published 2011
Copyright © Richard J. King 2011

Printed and bound in China by Eurasia

British Library Cataloguing in Publication Data
King, Richard J.
    Lobster. – (Animal)
    1. Lobsters. 2. Lobster culture. 3. Lobster fisheries.
    4. Lobster industry. 5. Cooking (Lobsters)
    I. Title II. Series
    641.3'95-DC22

ISBN 978 1 86189 795 4

Contents

1 What is a Lobster?

> The popularity of the Lobster extends far beyond the limits
> of our island, and he travels about to all parts of the known
> world, like an imprisoned spirit soldered up in an air-tight box.
> W. B. Lord, 1867[1]

I, for one, first came face to face with a live lobster at Main Line Seafood in suburban Ardmore, Pennsylvania. When I arrived on the first morning of my first summer job I thought the lobsters were staring at me from their tank. Their black eyes twitched and their antennae whiskered slowly but otherwise they sat menacingly still. They had piled on top of each other, backed into one corner in a rugby-style battle clump with their banded claws rested, in repose, yet seemingly eager to burst out and attack. The lobster tank had some algae growing on the glass, and I remember wondering if it would be more or less pathetic if we gave them some sand, a couple of rocks, maybe even a fake plant or two.

During my first summer I scrubbed fishcake pans most of the day but at the start of my second summer the owner promoted me to the counter. He prepared me for my new role by giving me a collared shirt and gripping my wrist to explain the most important thing for me to remember: 'Yes, ma'am! Just came in this morning.'

At Main Line Seafood we sold live lobsters from the tank at the front window. We also sold canned lobster meat, plastic containers of fresh lobster meat, frozen lobster tails, and we offered lobster rolls to the lunch-time crowd, which amounted to toasting a hot dog bun and dumping in some lobster meat

Kosti Ruohomaa, *Maine Lobster, Monhegan Island,* 1957, silver gelatin print.

on lettuce leaves, while a bag of frozen potatoes sizzled in the deep fryer.

Although the lobster species we sold, the American lobster (*Homarus americanus*), ranges naturally from North Carolina to Labrador, it was, and still is, primarily caught in traps by small collections of commercial fishermen along the coast and islands eastwards from New York City. The largest populations of these lobsters, and subsequently lobstermen, are off the Canadian Maritimes and the state of Maine. Offshore trawlers and trappers in the deep waters of the northwestern Atlantic dragged up lobsters from the bottom, and these creatures might have found their way into our tanks, cans and containers, too.

When I worked at Main Line Seafood in the late 1980s the lobster fishery in the Gulf of Maine and around the Maritimes was just beginning a period of massive growth after a relatively stable forty years or so. Since then landings have tripled in weight, with no sign of any significant abatement. James Acheson, a scholar of this industry, wrote:

> The Maine lobster fishery is one of the world's most successful fisheries. It is distinguished by a sense of stewardship, political support for conservation rules, and effective fisheries conservation legislation. In these respects, it is different from most other fisheries in the industrialized world.[2]

Gilbert's Lobsters in Pemaquid, Maine, 1938. Wherever you are in the world, eating lobster is as much about the experience, the event, as the flavour of the food.

Ranges of Major Commercial Lobster Species

Based on FAO 2008 global production in tonnes

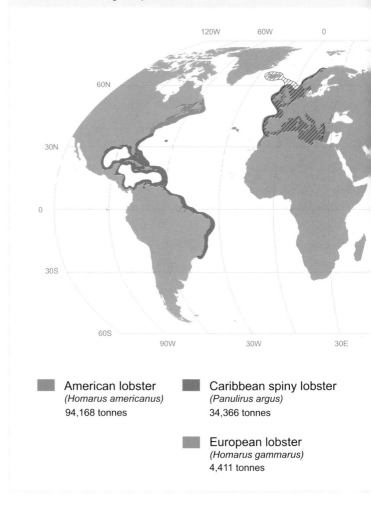

American lobster
(Homarus americanus)
94,168 tonnes

Caribbean spiny lobster
(Panulirus argus)
34,366 tonnes

European lobster
(Homarus gammarus)
4,411 tonnes

Ranges of the seven most productive commercial lobster fisheries in 2008, from FAO statistics and L. B. Holthuis et al., 1991/2006. (Biologists have found *J. edwardsii* and *novaehollandiae* to be the same species genetically.)

120E   180   120W

60N

30N

0

30S

60S

90E   150E   150W

/// **Norway lobster**
     (Nephrops norvegicus)
     72,548 tonnes

     Western rock lobster
     (Panulirus cygnus)
     8,961 tonnes

     Southern rock lobster
     (Jasus edwardsii / novaehollandiae)
     6,858 tonnes

Schnur 2010

I left Main Line Seafood after my second summer, heading off to university. Though my mother had occasionally ordered lobster for a special occasion while I was growing up, I never ordered this at restaurants myself because of disinterest (and the price). I didn't properly eat lobster meat until I was in my twenties when a friend invited me to his family's summer home in Maine. One foggy evening we ate fresh lobster on the dock. My friend's family taught me the intricacies of how to eat the animal, such as how to suck the meat from the legs and how to find the orange unfertilized roe in the female. With fresh salted corn and cold bottled beer that lobster was sweet and had a perfect texture. The smell of butter blended with that of the low tide and the exposed, popping rockweed. Eating lobster is as much about the experience as it is the taste itself. We sat with our feet dangling over the water, flicking the shells back from where they came. John Steinbeck said it better in *Travels with Charley* (1962):

> Those dark-shelled Maine lobsters from the dark water which are the best lobsters in the world . . . There are no lobsters like these – simply boiled, with no fancy sauces, only melted butter and lemon, they have no equals anywhere. Even shipped or flown alive away from their dark homes, they lose something.[3]

Years later I served as a sternman for a few seasons aboard the lobsterboat *Whistler*, out of Noank, Connecticut, fishing the eastern waters of Long Island Sound. I was a part-timer, going out a few days a week in the warmer months. Lobster fishing is enormously satisfying. I relished the steam out to the fishing grounds, the curiosity of what's going to be in the trap each time it breaks the surface, the seabirds, the sunrises, the earned exhaustion, the watching of the other boats, the yarn-spinning when baiting-up at the dock, and the flavour of black coffee in a paper cup after hard work on the salt water. I liked eating for dinner the food we'd caught that morning. It doesn't escape me, however, that it's easy to love a job when you're a part-timer, working on a wage – when your livelihood doesn't depend on it.

My boss was Captain John Whittaker, a tall man who has been fishing for over 35 years. He lives in the house in which he was raised. His father was a boat builder who constructed wooden craft on the same ground where John stacks and maintains his gear. Whittaker has relatives in lobster-rich Nova Scotia and his wife, Elizabeth, is from Maine and is the daughter and sister of men who have made their living in the lobster business. Whittaker keeps photo albums of boats and local history, and he enjoys reading maritime nonfiction in the evening. He is a patient man, rarely drinks and rarely curses, preferring expressions like 'Holy crow!' He calls lobsters 'bugs'.

Whittaker looks out each morning on his own dock when he has breakfast. Lobstering is one of the few commercial fisheries these days that allows a person to sleep at home at night. He runs his own rusty old railway to winch his boat out of the water, and he has a refrigerated shipping container to store bait. Between and around his driveway, the dock and up the small hill to his house, are piles of old and less-old gear – barrels, coils of rope, stacks of traps and plastic totes, buckets of nylon bait bags – and a variety of other items that his wife might call junk, such as rotting boats, split buoys and a dead outboard engine. Though his bait barrels stink and his diesel engine starts rumbling and smoking often before daybreak, his neighbours like having him there, because they can buy the freshest, cheapest lobster right off the boat.

Whittaker is one of the few people in the area who fishes year round, usually by himself in frigid winters, but he also needs to

Different species of clawed, spiny, and slipper lobsters, as well as other decapods, in this plate from John Jonston's *Historiae Naturalis de Quadrupedibus libri. Cum aeneis figures* (Amsterdam, 1657).

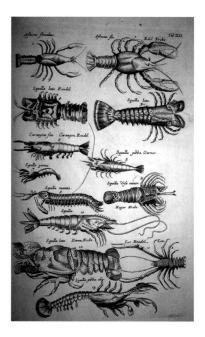

Ando Hiroshige, *Iseebi and Ebi* or *Lobster and Shrimp*, 1840, colour woodcut. This seems to depict the Japanese spiny lobster, *Panulirus japonicus*, the most common lobster in these waters, fished commercially.

supplement the family income – two of his daughters are in college – with other local work. He jokes regularly about ditching the lobster business and picking up farming or anything else. He has the skills to do a hundred other jobs, but he sticks with it. There is something in this catching of lobsters that is well beyond material gain.

The American lobster fished by John Whittaker, sold by Main Line Seafood, and eaten only on special occasions by my mother is not, however, the only lobster species worth catching, selling, eating – or reading about.

Though the American lobster is the best known and the most valuable lobster species commercially, for decades it has occupied less than 40 per cent of the world catch of lobsters by weight.[4] A species quite similar to the American lobster is the European lobster (*Homarus gammarus*), caught in the waters of northwestern Europe. Spiny lobsters (mostly *Panulirus cygnus*) have for many years been the highest-value fishery in Australia, worth AU$462 million in 2008–9, with the majority of the

Norway lobsters, *Nephrops norvegicus*, also known as prawns or scampi, caught in a commercial trawl in the Clyde, Scotland. The *Nephrops* fishery in the waters off northwestern Europe has grown immensely in recent decades.

product exported in various forms to China and Japan.[5] Ask for fresh lobster in a restaurant in the Bahamas and you'll get a plate of the Caribbean spiny lobster (*P. argus*), otherwise known as rock lobster or 'warm water' lobster, a significant fishery throughout the Caribbean. Recently I bought a 'cold water' lobster tail at a Japanese restaurant in Morro Bay, California, and was served, I believe, a delicious portion of a California spiny lobster (*P. interruptus*). The waiter was not certain. The United States imports spiny lobster from nearly fifty countries, including Taiwan, Oman, South Africa and Nicaragua. Brazil has regularly been the largest supplier.[6]

The simple question 'What is a lobster?' turns out to be complicated. How is it different from a crayfish? a prawn? a shrimp? or scampi? It is similar to travelling the English-speaking countries of the globe and asking 'What is a biscuit?' No clear-cut definition of lobster exists for biologists or linguists.

This is not a new problem. Aristotle wrote: 'With regard to the crustaceans, one species is that of the crayfish, and a second, resembling the first, is that of the lobster; the lobster differing from the crayfish in having large claws, and in a few other respects as well.'[7] It really depends on what part of the world you're in and whom you're asking. Most of the British know the spiny lobster of European waters (*Palinurus elephas*) as the crayfish or crawfish, while, for most Americans, these are common inclusive names for numerous smaller crustacean species that inhabit only fresh water. One scholar identified in 23 different countries 53 different names for *Nephrops norvegicus*, an important commercial species of the northeastern Atlantic and the North Sea, referred to most often as the Norway lobster, the Dublin Bay prawn, or scampi.[8] In Australia *Thenus orientalis* is known as the Shovel-nosed lobster or the Moreton Bay bug. Lobster krill are not actual lobsters by almost everyone's biological definition, nor are squat lobsters. I could go on. Not only are there language variations, but differences in common and regional names. Scientific nomenclature doesn't always make things easier: one genus is called *Palinurus*, one is *Panulirus*, and another *Palinurellus*. It also depends if your taxonomy is based on morphology or more recent genetic standards.

In 2006 the late great Dutch biologist Professor Lipke Bijdeley Holthuis, while updating with colleagues his report for the United Nations Food and Agriculture Organization, identified 149 species of lobster that were of interest or potential interest to fishermen around the world. I'll use his taxonomic nomenclature here.[9]

Everyone can agree that a lobster is an animal. Whittaker isn't far off in calling them bugs, because lobsters are related to insects in that they are also arthropod invertebrates with a segmented body, jointed legs and an external structure of some kind. The English word seems to have derived from this insect-like appearance, evolving through various forms and spellings from the original Latin word for locust, *locusta*.[10]

Everyone also agrees that a lobster, within the phylum Arthropoda, is an aquatic crustacean (think 'crusty'): it has no wings or neck, but has gills, two sets of antennae and a rigid exoskeleton. Taxonomists place lobsters under the order Decapoda, meaning 'ten feet'. As an adult, a lobster, unlike most shrimp and krill, is a poor swimmer, primarily crawling on the ocean bottom. A lobster has a fused head and thorax, the cephalothorax, under which are protected gills. It has an abdomen, called the tail if we're at the restaurant, under which are fan-like appendages called pleopods or 'swimmerets', and three sets of maxillipeds, 'jaw feet', that serve as mouth appendages to help still other mouthparts. Like a shrimp, a lobster's body tends to be more long than wide – as opposed to a crab,

Six different types of lobster as they appear in L. B. Holthuis's seminal *Marine Lobsters of the World* (1991). Just two decades later, modern decapod taxonomists, using phylogenetics, placed the polychelid lobsters in a different family and do not consider the mud lobster a lobster at all – more a shrimp.

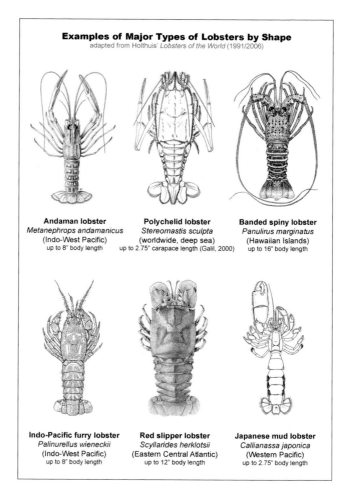

Examples of Major Types of Lobsters by Shape
adapted from Holthuis' *Lobsters of the World* (1991/2006)

Andaman lobster
Metanephrops andamanicus
(Indo-West Pacific)
up to 8" body length

Polychelid lobster
Stereomastis sculpta
(worldwide, deep sea)
up to 2.75" carapace length (Galil, 2000)

Banded spiny lobster
Panulirus marginatus
(Hawaiian Islands)
up to 16" body length

Indo-Pacific furry lobster
Palinurellus wieneckii
(Indo-West Pacific)
up to 8" body length

Red slipper lobster
Scyllarides herklotsii
(Eastern Central Atlantic)
up to 12" body length

Japanese mud lobster
Callianassa japonica
(Western Pacific)
up to 2.75" body length

whose abdomen has evolved to tuck under its cephalothorax. What different cultures consider a lobster fits into several different families within the Decapoda. Some lobsters have claws to protect themselves, some have spines and some make do with camouflage. Lobsters vary greatly in the shape of their exoskeleton, their behaviour, their habitat and their development.

For a workshop in Perth, Australia, Stanley Cobb and Bruce Phillips once assembled a dream team of lobster specialists, leading to a two-volume book titled *The Biology and Management of Lobsters* (1980). They state the matter of defining lobsters this way:

> The animals colloquially called lobsters, rock lobsters, or marine crayfish fall into several taxonomically distinct groups: the clawed lobsters (Nephropidae), the spiny lobsters (Palinuridae), the slipper lobsters (Scyllaridae), and the coral lobsters (Synaxidae). Despite the taxonomic differences, it seems appropriate to treat them together. As W. Herrnkind pointed out at the workshop, the lobster is a very significant biological entity. It is widely distributed, large in size, long lived, abundant, and ecologically consequential. Although lobsters are a morphologically diverse group composed of many species [Cobb and Phillips counted 163 at the time], the ecological differences between them are not great, and they appear to be physiologically quite similar.[11]

Professors Cobb and Phillips are still studying and publishing about these crustaceans and still attending international meetings devoted exclusively to their study. Crustacean taxonomists continue to change and debate lobster phylogeny. Yet right now, indifferent to scientific nomenclature, some fisherman

PRICE $4.50   JULY 28, 2008

THE
NEW YORKER

out there is licking his lips in anticipation of the food or money to be had from a catch of African spear lobsters (*Linuparus somniosus*) or Arabian whip lobsters (*Puerulus sewelli*) or Japanese spiny lobsters (*Panulirus japonicus*). Lobsters are crawling ocean bottoms all over the earth, from shallow pits in intertidal regions to waters almost 10,000 feet deep. Lobsters hunt in the frigid Arctic Ocean and amidst the tropical reefs of the South Pacific.[12] They breed around some of the most remote islands on earth, such as Easter Island and Tristan da Cunha. There have been lobster species that did not adapt fast enough and are now extinct, and there surely remain several species still undiscovered, flicking their antennae in a dim foreign ocean. The scientific community described in 1990, for example, the Musical furry lobster (*Palibythus magnificus*) from only a few specimens caught in deep water off Western Samoa.[13]

I examine here how marine biologists, explorers, fishermen, divers, cooks, epicures, humanities scholars and a variety of writers, filmmakers and artists have perceived the lobster. I focus primarily on the marine clawed lobsters of the Gulf of Maine and northern Europe, which Professor Holthuis and others refer to as the 'true lobsters', since these are most familiar to Western readers and are the lobsters most commonly represented in the arts. I seek to examine if there is indeed something special about our perception of the lobster – whether you see one through a snorkel mask, in a fisherman's trap, in a fishmonger's tank or on your fancy dinner plate. Why is it, after all, that we so often associate the lobster with decadence, sex and a lemon spritz of absurdity?

In this 2008 magazine cover illustration, titled *Summer Getaway*, Peter de Sève shows how we culturally associate the lobster with luxury, sex appeal and humour – alongside a slightly nervous awareness that we regularly boil these animals alive.

2 Dissecting a Bug

A lobster is monstrous to the eye the first time it is seen, but when we have been shown the use of the case, the color, the tentacula, and the proportion of the claws, and have seen that he has not a scale nor a bristle, nor any part, but fits exactly to some habit and condition of the creature; he then seems as perfect and suitable to his sea-house, as a glove to a hand.

Ralph Waldo Emerson, 1833[1]

When Professor Jonathan Geller was a graduate student he took a summer course in the town of Woods Hole, Massachusetts, renowned for its Marine Biological Laboratory and the Woods Hole Oceanographic Institution. He met a woman there, a fellow aspiring scientist, and asked her out to dinner. Young Geller, slender and earnest, thought he would treat his date to the most impressive meal he could offer, so he walked her to the Fishmonger Cafe and ordered two fresh local lobsters. When dinner arrived on the table, a sample of one of the largest extant species of crustaceans on earth, Geller could not resist approaching his dinner clinically. 'I gave her a lecture', he said. 'I thought it would be impressive, but after a lobster is boiled there isn't as much to see on the inside. So I was just really pulling the legs apart. She thought that was all kind of peculiar.'[2] As the summer wore on, she either forgot that evening or, more likely, embraced his eccentric enthusiasm. They married four years later.

Geller earned his PhD at the University of California and has since led dissections of hundreds of lobsters, crayfish, crabs and other marine invertebrates for over a thousand students of marine biology. When I met him he was teaching and conducting research at the Moss Landing Marine Laboratories, beside

Malcolm Cheape, *Lobster Sketch*, 2006, mixed water-based media collage.

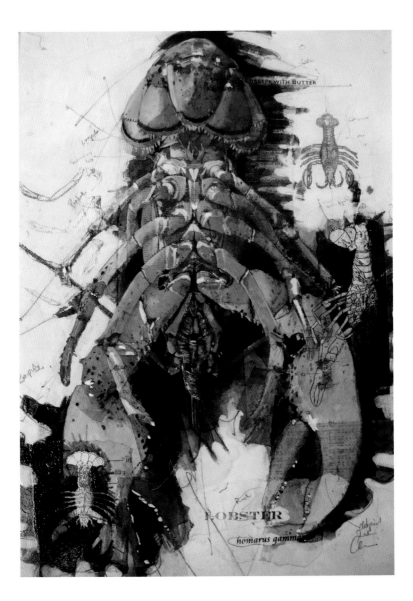

LOBSTER WITH BUTTER

LOBSTER

homarus gamma

Monterey Bay, California. He kindly agreed to do a lobster dissection for me.

To get a couple of specimens I went down the road from his lab to a fish market where they had bubbling tanks filled with lobsters. The fishmonger said he hadn't carried California spiny lobster for years, but they sold live Maine lobsters year round.

I asked: 'Are these all from Maine'?

'Yes, sir.'

'But those have "Canada Wild" printed on their claw bands.'

'Well, you know, sir, Maine curls around all the way up there. To Canada.'

Perhaps he was thinking of the Gulf of Maine, rather than the state, and, to be fair, the American lobster is often known as the Maine lobster. If you're in Canada, it's the Atlantic Canada lobster. I asked how long they had been in the tank.

'Just came in this morning.'

I requested one female and one male. To tell the difference between a male and female clawed lobster, you need to turn the animal upside down. Females have smaller claws and a wider abdomen, but the easier diagnosis is to find the two small appendages near where the thorax meets the abdomen, the first set of swimmerets. A female's pair is flat and feathery. The male's pair is relatively thin and rigid, effectively two half-cylinders that act as a penis for delivering spermatophores into an external pouch on the female. When mating, the male lobster places the two swimmerets together, as if praying, thus making an enclosed tube to deliver. The female lobster uses these gametes to fertilize her eggs when she excretes them, sometimes more than a year later. Older, larger females often lay two sets of eggs with one deposit of sperm.[3]

Spiny lobster females store their spermatophores in an open area in the same anatomical region as their clawed cousins. As opposed to those of the males, the swimmerets of spiny females are branched. Spiny males have an especially long second pair of legs. Another way to gender a spiny lobster is to observe the aftermost set of legs: if these have little hook-like structures at the tips, you've got a female. The females use the hooks to open up their 'tar-spot', the colloquial name for the external package of spermatophores.

Each lobster weighed about a pound and a half. I gasped at the price. The fishmonger said he purchased them regularly from a company in San Francisco that flies them across the country. I packed the lobsters on ice in a cooler and returned to the lab.

Professor Geller speaks softly. He pronounces taxonomical nomenclature with ease, can say the word anaesthetize aloud without lisping or tripping over it, and he weaves in beautiful technical vocabulary such as crypsis, a more exacting term for camouflage, and autotomize, which is the verb for when animals such as the lobster sacrifice a claw to escape a greater danger. Geller pronounces carapace, the exoskeleton covering the fused head and thorax of the lobster, to rhyme with grace, declaiming the word slowly as if it were a little poem. Yet Geller is anything but pretentious. He wears jeans, running shoes and uses the phrase 'narc-ed out' to describe the lethargic state of a lobster after freezing. He defines a lobster elegantly: 'It is a common name for any stout, heavily-armoured, marine, bottom-crawling decapod.'

Geller put the female lobster, narc-ed out from the ice, on a dissection tray. He brought out a preserved specimen of both a spiny and a slipper lobster, and placed them alongside. 'When you turn all three of these over and look underneath you see that anatomically there's not much difference. It's mainly in the shape of the antennae and in the number and size of the

In response to
hurricane events
off the Florida
coast, Caribbean
spiny lobsters,
Panulirus argus,
migrate in single-
file lines.

chelipeds.' Chelipeds are legs with claws at the end. 'For the
slipper lobster you can see that its carapace is expanded later-
ally. Into a flat shield. It's as if it were made of rubber and
someone just stretched it all out. Even a pair of its antennae
has evolved to be flat shields. As a defence, slipper lobsters go
more for armour and crypsis.'

Lobsters use their two pairs of antennae as feelers, like bee-
tles, to probe their way around and to gather information. The
smaller pair, which is branched on several lobster species, is less
for touch and more for identifying chemicals in the ocean for
feeding and socializing, for interpreting their environment and
cues from other lobsters in a sensory form that is similar to an
underwater mixture of taste and smell. With chemosensory
neurons, lobsters can discern between other lobsters, respond to
sexual signals and identify various other waterborne intricacies.[4]

Perhaps due to claw-envy, an adult spiny lobster's primary
antennae, depending on the species, can grow larger than 46
cm (18 inches), more than twice the length of this book. These

The Royal slipper
lobster, *Arctides
regalis*, in the
waters of Hawaii.
The primary pair
of the slipper
lobster's antennae
has evolved to
be short and flat-
tened, leading to
another common
name: the shovel-
nosed lobster.

Electron microscope magnification of the first walking leg of an American lobster, *Homarus americanus*, revealing the number and variety of *setae*.

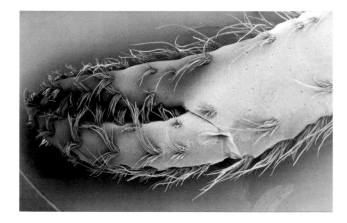

antennae are thick and prickly, like little clubs or horns, which can taper to delicate, thread-like tips. Holding the preserved specimen Geller said: 'The spiny-ness of these antennae cannot be underestimated. Imagine this guy in a crevice, facing out. See how these spines are angled to also face out? It would be difficult to reach in there without shredding your hand.' Biologists think the Caribbean spiny lobster uses its antennae to stay in step during mass migrations. These lobsters may travel for perhaps as far as fifty miles in a single-file 'superhighway' of thousands of individuals, remaining in contact using their antennae, as if each probing with blind canes, thus keeping in touch with the lobster in front and reducing drag as they march their way to preferred waters.[5]

To aid with gathering information lobster shells and appendages sprout thousands of sensitive hair-like setae that help the antennae with the lobster's chemosensory work and sense of motion. The setae help catch plankton and may also aid females with tending and grooming their fertilized eggs under the abdomen.[6]

Geller picked up the American lobster to examine its compound eyes, which each contains some 13,500 reflective mirror-like facets.[7] Author Trevor Corson put it poetically: 'The eye of the lobster is of such novel and ingenious design that it inspires religious faith and scientific admiration alike.'[8] Lobsters are nocturnal and live in the dark ocean bottom, crawling between rocks, coral and other crevices. Their eyes have evolved to function well in low light and to detect movement, but they are not as effective at discerning colour or identifying shapes.[9] The eyes of clawed and spiny lobsters are on stalks for a 360-degree view, yet they can still quickly retract under their shell.

Lobsters migrate, tunnel and dig. They move sand, mud and stones to carve out protected dens, to which they can return and hide stashes of food. Lobsters respond to subtle changes in water pressure, currents and light. American lobsters seem to even respond specifically to the autumnal equinox and the winter solstice.[10] And recent studies suggest that the Caribbean spiny lobster might be one of the only invertebrates we've identified so far that can navigate using the earth's magnetism. For one experiment in the Florida Keys biologists caught a group of these lobsters, loaded them in water-filled containers into trucks and suspended these containers inside the truck with ropes, surrounding them with magnets. (I'm not making this up.) They drove around in 'a series of erratic turns and circles', and before they put the lobsters back in the water at two sites, dozens of miles from where they were lifted off the sandy bottom, the scientists covered the lobsters' eyestalks with little rubber caps. A convincing majority of the lobsters turned and walked in the direction of where they were first kidnapped.[11]

Geller pointed toward the tiny sacs at the base of the specimen's antennae, which regulate its equilibrium, helping the animal float right side up.[12] These sacs infuse microscopic grains

A large male California spiny lobster, *Panulirus interruptus*, resting in its shelter during the day.

of sand that stick and weigh on hundreds of minute hairs within. Lobsters can detect slight changes in temperature and salinity, essential factors to their growth, moulting, migration and reproduction. Clawed lobsters seem to be capable of making and detecting small noises, and the Caribbean lobster, like others spinys, has evolved a file-like pad that rubs against a raised ridge at the base of its antennae to make a sound, probably for mating communication or defence.[13] One biologist described this underwater noise as 'comparable to that of a moist finger rubbed against a window pane'.[14]

Since at least the eighteenth century there has been speculation as to the lobster's sensitivity to loud noises, or at least the accompanying vibrations. In August of 1777 William Eddis, a seemingly trustworthy correspondent, wrote that huge lobsters lived in the brackish East and Hudson Rivers around Manhattan. Eddis explained that the Revolutionary War affected the creatures in the water: 'Lobsters, of a prodigious size, were, till of late, caught in vast numbers, but it is a fact, surprising as it may appear, that, since the late incessant cannonading, they have entirely forsaken the coast, not one having been taken, or seen, since the commencement of hostilities.'[15] Professor Geller and John Whittaker are sceptical, but some contemporary lobstermen have claimed that after a night of fireworks the lobsters all go into hiding.[16]

Geller put the female lobster he planned to dissect on its belly with its tail toward him, the 'Wild Canada' bands remaining around its claws. The American lobster is nearly identical to the European lobster genetically and morphologically, just larger and thicker on average and possessing a little ventral tooth underneath the rostrum. The rostrum is the projection of shell between the lobster's eyes, a flat spiked tusk known to fishermen in the UK as the 'beak'. The American and European lobsters both evolved, like all of the lobster species, from a common ancestor that scurried on the ocean's bottom over 250 million years ago (or millions of years earlier still if you choose the earliest decapods as their progenitors).[17] The clawed lobsters seem to have emerged similar to their present state some 150

American lobsters with natural shell colours of calico, blue, and split brown and red. These extremely rare colours tend to stay with the animals throughout their lives.

In 1719 French naturalist Louis Renard illustrated a few lobster species from his travels in maritime Southeast Asia. Though he seems to have painted here the Ornate spiny lobster (*Panulirus ornatus*), his description is of a 'Mountain Crayfish', which, he writes above, is caught in the woods, climbs trees, can be 3–4 feet long, and is very good to eat. Renard writes that they lay eggs in the sand (pictured lower right).

million years ago, sharing the Jurassic oceans with ichthyosaurs and plesiosaurs. These clawed lobsters then probably evolved well over a hundred million years later into separate species with different ranges on either side of the North Atlantic.[18]

Both the American and European lobster have a relatively smooth mottled brown shell to blend into the rocks and seaweed. Some claim the American lobster is more green-brown while the European lobster dons on average more of a blue-black coat. Lobstermen on both sides of the Atlantic have hauled up exceptionally rare lobsters that are royal blue, red, yellow, pitch black, albino and a variety of mixtures, all a result of genetic pigment mutations. Very occasionally a clawed lobster is caught whose colour is split right down the middle like a practical joke, typically red on one side and the normal olive-brown on the other. A rare shell colour usually remains for the lobster's adult life, regardless of the number of moults, although temperature and the ocean bottom can affect the pigment, too. According to Diane Cowan, the founder of The Lobster Conservancy, who has been dubbed the Jane Goodall of the American lobster, you can make a lobster blue by feeding it squid. You can also make a clawed lobster red, of course, by boiling it, which breaks down

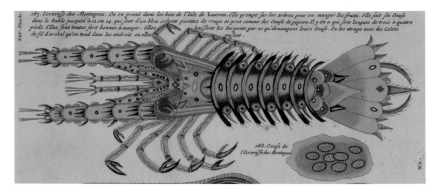

the proteins in its shell pigment, the same process that occurs when cooking any crustacean.[19]

Spiny lobsters are the glorious ones when it comes to colour, with species exhibiting dazzling hues, and enough stripes and spots to rival the jazziest tropical fish. The Painted spiny lobster (*Panulirus versicolor*) of the western Pacific and Indian Ocean has pink and white antennae and electric blue stripes along its legs, swimmerets and tail. Bright markings in lobsters tend to occur in warmer, shallower waters and are connected perhaps to mate attraction, although at least one biologist believes that a parallel row of spots might help them stay in line when migrating.[20] The colours of spiny lobsters inspired artists of early natural history expeditions, painters such as Louis Renard and Olivia Frances Tonge. In 1867 British author and naturalist W. B. Lord wrote:

The coral reefs fringing the islands of Mauritius afford shelter to members of the family of *Palinurus*, which in both size and splendour of colouring far excel those taken in our seas. Some . . . looked so much like works of art that we could almost fancy Pallisey, that king of potters, must have returned to life, and that these were some of his choicest productions. Some were of delicate sea-green banded with white and ultra-marine blue, alternately. Others were striped with pale yellow, black, and green, whilst all were so highly glazed, and carried such a brilliant polish, that we deeply regretted the perishable nature of living things.[21]

Professor Geller wiped his hands on a towel. He grasped the American lobster's two large front claws, calling attention to their asymmetry. The right was a crusher claw and the left a

The Painted spiny lobster, *Panulirus versicolor*, or in French 'Langouste barriolée', crawling the reefs off Papua New Guinea.

pincher claw. The crusher is also known in the US and the UK as the cracker, thumb or knobbed claw. The pincher is synonymous with pincer, cutter, seizer, decorative, toothed or quick claw. The crusher and pincher claws are not always on the same sides of the lobster. Biologists do not think this is genetic but determined in postlarval stages by environmental factors and chance. Geller knew of a few recorded instances in the wild where lobsters developed two pinchers or two crushers. Normally, once the sides and type of the claws are fixed in larvae, the same type of claw will grow back on the same side after each moult, even after autotomy.[22] As lobsters grow larger and older, the claws grow faster than the rest of their body, changing from about 5 per cent of their total weight in early larval stages to nearly half for the old bully males.[23]

Geller explained that the design of the tendons and muscles in a lobster claw has evolved to keep it closed, particularly the crusher type, thus increasing the force of its grip to hold on to crabs and crack the shell of a clam or a mussel. In other words, it is difficult for a fish, another lobster or your finger to stop the claw from closing but, at the same time, it's not terribly hard to stop the lobster from *opening* its claws – an easy task for, say, a stiff rubber band. Geller compared the separate functions of these claws to the evolution of vertebrate teeth. The pincher claw has sharp denticles for tearing while the molars of the crusher claw are for mashing and holding. The pincher claw has more setae and more fast-twitch fibres. I can tell you that when you put your hand into a lobster trap, into a pile of clacking, glistening lobsters that have only just broken the surface of the ocean, the type of claw that is going to nab your finger, even through a thick rubber glove, and make you yelp between clenched teeth, will be the pincher. The pincher throws the jab; the crusher inflicts the vice. When lobsters battle each other on the ocean bottom and the fight gets serious, they each usually find the other's crusher, regardless of which side it is on. The two crushers lock and hold until the weaker animal loses the claw or shows subservience.[24]

Sometimes aboard *Whistler* when we hauled up a string of traps that were full of lobsters, a few of them would grab on to another's claw or wrist or tail, usually with their pincher. We could only get them apart by sticking a flat metal gauge between a claw and turning it sideways, or sometimes we dunked the lobsters in the tank, which seemed to distract them enough to release. If we forced the two clenched lobsters apart too roughly or at too drastic an angle, one or both of them would autotomize – always at the same joint at the base of the carapace, where it clots immediately. For the fisherman, this loss of claw can be the difference of two or three dollars per bug. An asymmetrical lobster looks less appetizing on a dinner plate, and some prefer claw meat to tail meat. At the market when a lobster has only one claw it's called a 'cull'.

In 1895 the first and most accomplished of American lobsterologists, Francis Hobart Herrick, PhD, ScD, published his seminal book-length report for the United States Commission of Fish and Fisheries, which he revised as *Natural History of the American Lobster* (1911). Though most of what Herrick learned and described has been added to, little has been repudiated. His writings and illustrations remain a significant resource. Herrick is the Da Vinci, the Darwin, the William Shakespeare of lobster biology. He wrote at a time when a dash of lyricism or

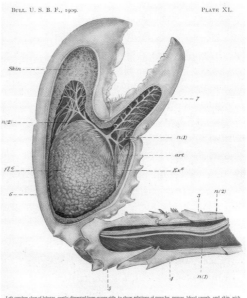

BULL. U. S. B. F., 1909.   PLATE XI.

Francis Hobart Herrick's illustration of a partially dissected American lobster's left crusher claw, from his *Natural History of the American Lobster* (1911).

Left crusher claw of lobster, partly dissected from upper side, to show relations of muscles, nerves, blood vessels, and skin, with principal branches of claw arteries and nerves laid bare. *art*, large artery which supplies both muscles of claw, and breaks into a regular system of branches in fine meat of tips; *n* (*1*), *n* (*2*), posterior and anterior nerve trunks supplying, respectively, the extensor (*Ex⁶*) and thumb, and the flexor (*fl⁶*) and index.

anthropomorphism didn't reflect poorly on a scientist. In his chapter on 'The Great Forceps', Herrick wrote:

> The big claws of the lobster are remarkable organs whether considered in the light of their structure, their development, or the process of their renewal, and the more we study them the more remarkable they appear. In most of the higher Crustacea the great claws are the chief weapons for both attack and defense and very efficient means for seizing and rending the prey, as well as for grasping and holding the female in the act of pairing.[25]

Professor Geller took his hands off the claws and folded the lobster gently. He pointed to the space where the carapace meets the segmented abdomen. Here is where the lobster will back out of its shell, to escape in order to grow. Lobsters must moult to get larger since their shell is rigid. For the first five years of the American lobster's life it moults approximately 25 times, then sheds its shell twice a year until it reaches sexual maturity, which is usually between five and eight years.[26] Once an adult, a male lobster tends to moult once a year, a female every other year, with both genders slowing down as they age. Moulting is affected by season, water temperature, salinity, mate availability, diet and other social and environmental conditions.

Geller said: 'When this lobster moults, it will split here at this suture site and back itself out. Then it has to pull all the appendages out the narrowest points. You can see how the claw has to pull through this slot here. Look how small that is.' A lobster will starve itself to prepare for moulting. Biologists believe it crawls to a protected place, since during the process and immediately afterward it will be immensely vulnerable. 'The muscles are really limp and watery so they can be squeezed. The animal is weak. It's a hard problem to solve, because it has to have enough strength to pull itself out, but the muscles can't be so well formed. Moulting can be the cause of death, a loss of claw, or the lobster could even get stuck.'

In 1875 Norwegian zoologist G. O. Sars described a European lobster in the moulting process off the coast of Tananger:

> It had just been taken out of a lobster-box [a submerged storage container] and could be handled without offering the slightest resistance. The shell on its back was burst in the middle, and the tail and the feet were nearly all out of the old shell, while the largest claw only stuck out half its length. This latter portion of the change of shell is evidently very dangerous, and although I observed it for quite a while, I could see little or no progress. It is certainly a painful and dangerous process, and probably many a lobster loses its life through it. Immediately after the changing of the shell the lobster is lean and miserable.[27]

Mature females usually copulate immediately after shedding their shell. After a lobster of either gender has moulted, it starts eating and filling its body with water so that the new shell will harden around a larger form. In a single moult the American lobster can increase its volume by more than 50 per cent and its length by more than 15 per cent.[28] Studies suggest the lobster will devour some of its own discarded shell, replacing some of the nutrients to rebuild. It generally takes weeks to fully harden its shell again.[29]

When fishing in the waters of Long Island Sound, if we hauled up a recently moulted legal lobster, called a 'shedder', we brought it back to the dock and used special loose rubber bands that would not cut into its claws, yet would still be in place when the shell hardened. We put shedders in a cage underneath the water until they were rigid enough to send to market. In parts of the world you can purchase 'soft-shelled' lobsters during certain weeks of the year.

'All right, let's look at the mouth', Geller said. With a dissecting probe he clicked on the hard teeth inside the lobster's mandibles. Even in its narc-ed state out of the water, the lobster's appendages fanned and gathered toward the mouth. Though one of the lobster's defining characteristics is that it has three sets of maxillipeds, it also has three additional sets of appendages above, also around the mouth. Each of these six appendages is nearly impossible to discriminate for the non-specialist – don't bother if you're trying to impress someone on a first date – as these appendages are all branched and overlapping, appearing to be twice as many. Some look like little gills and others like legs, and all of them nibble around in their devotion to the primary business of macerating and gathering from the sea what the large claws have torn and crushed or what happens to be floating past.

Lobsters are omnivorous. They eat what is available on the bottom. As one Welsh fisherman put it, lobsters eat 'anything with flesh on it, that has once lived'.[30] Lobsters eat (preferably living) marine worms, mussels, clams, fish, sea stars, sea urchins, octopus, squid, crabs, plankton, algae, sea grasses and decomposing organic matter of all kinds. The lobstermen of Western Australia have been fond of mixing with their baitfish a bullock hock, a piece of cattle hide and even a spot of kangaroo meat.[31] Occasionally lobsters devour each other. Herrick wrote: 'Lobsters are cannibals from birth, owing, primarily, to their strong instinct of pugnacity. The small, as well as the large, are ever ready to prey upon those still smaller and weaker than themselves.'[32]

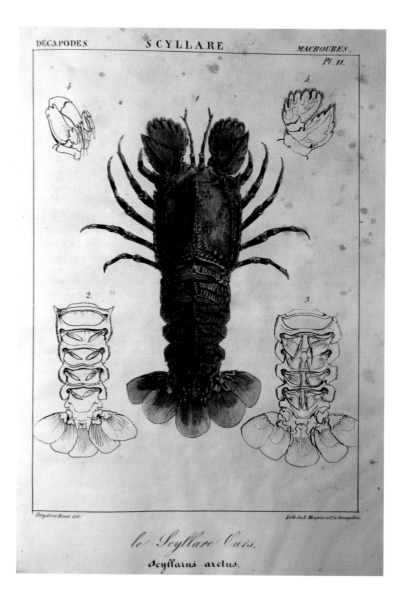

le Scyllare Ours.

Scyllarus arctus.

A lobsterman fans out the tail fins, or uropods, of an American lobster. Biologically, just these fins make up the true tail of the lobster; the rest of what we call the tail in a restaurant, the meat, is the animal's abdomen.

Geller turned the lobster around. He explained that the true tail of the lobster is only the set of four fins, the uropods, at the end of the abdomen on either side of the telson, which is the rigid middle plate between these four fins. He held the specific uropod where American and Canadian lobstermen would notch out a 'v' with a knife to mark that this female has had eggs recently.

The lobster began to wake up a little. 'This tail flipping behaviour is a neurological hallmark', Geller said. 'It's an escape response. If this were in water it would go jetting backwards.' Except in a larval form, nearly every species of lobster, besides crawling forward, can only flip itself in reverse through the water, which is most useful as it expertly backs into a shelter – seemingly without looking. The swimmerets under the abdomen help the lobster move forward when it is crawling high on its legs, but they are too small to be especially effective. The swimmerets are better for clearing out sand or holding and aerating eggs.

An illustration by Polydore Roux in his *Crustacés de la Méditerranée et de son littoral...* (1828) of a female *Scyllarus arctus*, the Small European locust lobster. In the line drawings of the underside of the abdomen, the male is left (2), and the female right (3).

Linguists and authors have enjoyed the lobster's characteristic of essentially only being able to swim backwards. The French word for the clawed lobster, *homard*, Milne-Edwards's genus name *Homarus* (Latinizing the French) and the German and Norwegian word *hummer* all might have their roots in the Old Norse verb *homa*, meaning to go backwards.[33] In the seventeenth century Jean de La Fontaine seized on the metaphor, beginning his Aesop-inspired fable 'The Lobster and Her Daughter' this way:

> The wise, sometimes, as lobsters do,
> To gain their ends back foremost go.
> It is the rower's art; and those
> Commanders who mislead their foes,
> Do often seem to aim their sight
> Just where they don't intend to smite.[34]

Geller stroked the flesh of the underside of the tail to make it curl. 'What is especially cool is that to do this tail flip response, there is really just one large nerve to control this huge muscle. The nerve runs down ventrally, longitudinally. Otherwise there's nothing inside this abdomen beyond muscle and intestine, which comes out here. This is the anus just underneath the telson.'

To begin the actual dissection Geller used a small pair of surgeon's scissors to cut a square out of the female's carapace, beginning aft where the animal would crawl out of its shell. I asked him about the ethics here, of dissecting a live lobster.

'With an invertebrate you can anaesthetize them or relax them. Often we use magnesium chloride, which debilitates their muscles. It's really hard to know what they're sensing. You have to be honest about that. You don't know. They have a small brain. There's no question they perceive, well, irritation. You give them

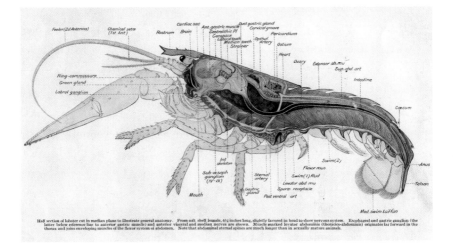

Half section of lobster cut in median plane to illustrate general anatomy. From soft shell female, 6¼ inches long, slightly layered in head to show nervous system. Esophageal and gastric ganglion (the latter below reference line to anterior gastric muscle) and anterior visceral and median nerves are shown. Muscle marked levator abdominis (thoracico-abdominis) originates far forward in the thorax and joins enveloping muscles of the flexor system of abdomen. Note that abdominal sternal spines are much longer than in sexually mature animals.

a stimulus and they respond. But pain? It depends how you define pain. It's definitely nervous irritation, a response.'

The lobster showed no reaction to the cut in its shell. Geller pointed to the exposed heart, a white rectangular bag that pulsed visibly. He explained that the circulatory system is primitive, an 'open system' without veins. There are holes in the heart that pump a watery, greenish fluid into arteries and across all of the body parts, bathing the organs under the carapace. As he cut into the shell, fluid leaked onto the tray. This blood is the white, creamy substance that rises to the surface when boiling a lobster.[35]

Geller continued to cut open the carapace, adroitly pulling the shell from the connective tissue, which revealed a red-flecked, film-like material. This would have been the new shell when the lobster moulted. Forward of the heart and about four times the size was the stomach. This two-part organ is ridged like a baleen hoop-dress and has three hard molars on the inside, serving a

Francis Hobart Herrick's 1911 'Half section of lobster cut in median plane to illustrate general anatomy' remains both accurate and useful a century later.

purpose like a bird's rock-filled gizzard. The lobster's stomach not only grinds and sifts food but also stores material. Herrick wrote of the lobster's stomach when discussing recently moulted specimens: 'I have found soft lobsters with their stomachs stuffed full of the shells of mollusks and other calcareous fragments, actions which point clearly to the need of the animals at such times to obtain a supply of lime as quickly as possible.'[36]

Professor Geller cut a wider opening in the shell up to the rostrum and showed the digestive glands, which, if cooked, would remain soft and the colour of the inside of an avocado. This is gastronomically known as the 'tomalley' or 'the mustard'.

Geller next touched his probe to the brain, a white nub of tissue about the size of the tip of a ballpoint pen. 'That's about as big as it is. That little bulge there.' The lobster has a dozen other smaller nodes of nerve tissue, but this brain, according to neurobiologist Barbara Beltz (who also calls it the supraesophageal ganglion), is 'generally concerned with primary processing of visual, chemosensory, and mechanosensory inputs, as well as higher-order processing and integration of these modalities'.[37] By touching a white stringy nerve beside this ganglion Geller elicited a twitch from one of the antennae, but by then the heart was barely moving. He assumed the lobster was now 'brain-dead' due to lack of circulation.

Snipping the carapace further, Geller revealed that the gills are outside the body cavity on both sides of the lobster – under the carapace, but separated by a thin wall. The lobster's feathery gills and their paired fan-like parts, which serve to draw in salt water, are actually branches formed out of the base of the legs, as if we had breathing apparatus on our upper thigh. The in-flow of water facilitates the movement of blood across the gills – the exchange of oxygen and carbon dioxide. The water is then expelled out of both sides of the lobster's head. Geller pointed

A female American lobster with fertilized eggs, known as 'berried'. A v-notch has been clipped from its uropod, a message to fellow fishermen that this individual has recently been captured with eggs – so throw it back in the water.

out the two bladders that connect to a set of pores at the base of each antenna, from which the lobster urinates. The seawater flowing forward from the gills can send this urine several feet in front of its body, allowing it to communicate a variety of social functions. Trevor Corson described the process: 'Quite possibly, lobsters [are] sensing each other and sending signals – "I beat you up last night, remember?" or "Would you like to mate with me, I'm about to get undressed?" – by pissing in each other's faces.'[38]

The last thing Professor Geller examined during this dissection was an unexpected find underneath this female's carapace: a long dark-green organ with little yellow specks. It had two lobes and rested dorsally on either side of the heart, extending underneath the shell of the abdomen. It was a well-developed ovary packed with eggs. If the cooked lobster Geller dissected for his future wife had been a fertile adult female, he would have found this as dense, bright orange roe. Chef Jasper White, author of an entire cookbook on preparing lobster, uses these cooked lobster eggs, the 'coral', to 'add little bursts of flavor and texture to sauces and soups'.[39]

Beginning as a small white glob, a mature female's ovary develops eggs for a good part of a year until the organ turns dark green and expands to crowd the upper part of the lobster under the shell – from behind the eyes to well inside the abdomen.[40] When ready, the female lobster secretes the eggs and releases the previously deposited sperm to fertilize. Herrick wrote, rather excitedly: 'The crustacean sperm . . . is like a submarine torpedo, loaded and primed, capable of piercing the membrane and forcing a passage into the egg the moment its latent energy is set free.'[41]

Francis Hobart Herrick's paintings of the first and fourth larval stages of the American lobster, from his 1895 monograph *The American Lobster: A Study of its Habits and Development*.

Herrick found, depending on the size and age of the female, that an American lobster can carry anywhere from a few thousand to nearly a hundred thousand eggs.[42] The lobster Geller dissected was carrying several thousand. In the wild the female lobster arranges the fertilized eggs underneath the abdomen, held in clumps by a cement-like substance on the swimmerets. The female carries these fertilized eggs for another nine to eleven months until the lobster larvae hatch at night, floating to the surface to a planktonic start to life.[43] Thus the entire gestation period for a lobster can be almost two years.

Each tiny American or European lobster larva, now open to predation and subject to wind and tides, will as it moults transform itself over the course of about four to eight weeks, depending mostly on water temperature, into four distinctly different, gradually larger, swimming forms. If by enormous odds it survives life as plankton it will develop to look like a tiny

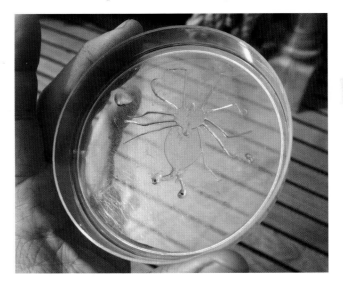

Lobster phyllosoma caught in a plankton net in the Straits of Florida, 2010.

Illustration of a phyllosoma larva of the Common spiny lobster of Europe, *Palinurus elephas* [then *vulgaris*], by German scientist and artist Ernst Haeckel, 1904. Haeckel wrote: 'The common spiny lobster [*Languste*] . . . goes through a series of remarkable metamorphoses when it is young; the strange larva depicted here appears as a thin, round, glass-like transparent disc, bearing no resemblance to the adult . . . this larva was earlier described as a separate genus *Phyllosoma*.'

baby lobster. Then it will sink to the ocean bottom to hide and feed within the protection of a safer substrate, such as gravel or dense seaweed.

While putting away the preserved specimens Geller explained that spiny and slipper lobsters evolved to have a much shorter egg gestation – usually just a few weeks or months – yet the young of these species spend months and even years in a transparent larval form called a phyllosoma ('leaf body'), which can grow to be the size of a credit card. These larval lobster species then change into another form in order to settle to the bottom and grow into adults. The Western rock lobster, for example, transitions through a planktonic phyllosoma stage that can last almost a year and may float some 2,000 miles offshore into the Indian Ocean. Some might even settle on the coast of Africa.[44] A coral lobster of the West Indies, *Palinurellus gundlachi*, develops through a dozen different stages before becoming an adult.[45]

Various larvae of spiny lobsters are so large and ornate that they were interpreted by naturalists up until the twentieth century as their own species, just as caterpillars were not first associated with butterflies.[46]

After Professor Geller finished the dissection, as we were cleaning up, I told him that I planned to boil the lobsters straight away. Would he accept them for dinner?

'Absolutely. Thank you,' he said. 'My wife will appreciate these.'

3 Ancient, Giant and Plentiful

The wave-horses [ships] run over the fields of lobster.
Norse Saga, c. 12th century[1]

The legend goes this way: a North Sea gale on 29 October, 370 CE, tossed around a small wooden craft carrying seventeen monks, three nuns, the Abbot Regulus and a holy box containing a selection of the bones of a dead fisherman, the apostle St Andrew. They had set sail some two years earlier from Greece on a mission inspired by a divine vision. As the pitiless gale wore on, the pilgrims steered toward what appeared through wind-whipped sheets of water to be some sort of harbour – but with the seas erupting, the best they could do, exhausted, was to bash their boat to splinters on the shore near the mouth of a brook, barely swimming to safety while clutching the box of relics. With the vessel destroyed and the pilgrims shipwrecked, Regulus decided God wanted him to stay put. Later known as St Rule, the Abbot Regulus reportedly lived another thirty years, helping to establish a Christian stronghold that became a popular destination for pilgrims of the Middle Ages. This town would be named St Andrews, Scotland, and if it is not the most ancient little lobster port in the British Isles, it is certainly a village today where you can learn and see practically everything there is to know about lobsters and our historic relationship to these crustaceans.[2]

On the hill just up from where his boat might have been wrecked stands St Rule's Tower. It is square-sided and about 33

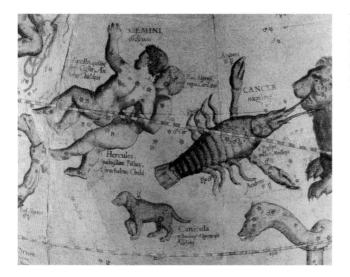

The lobster as Cancer, between Gemini and Leo, in the celestial globe drawn by Gerard Mercator, 1551.

metres (108 feet) high, seemingly erected in the twelfth century or earlier as part of the church to hold those alleged bones of St Andrew.[3] The stone remnants and ruins and foundations of more than a millennium's worth of cathedrals, churches, castles, homes, schools, walls, wells, graveyards, dungeons, turrets and towers overlook the ocean from atop this hill. Many of these early stone structures are now windswept, guano-pitted and crumbling into the edge of the sandstone cliffs.

If you climb to the top of St Rule's Tower, up a narrow spiral of steps inside, you can see an old pier that extends into St Andrews Bay and toward the North Sea. This pier is famous because on Sundays a group of undergraduates wearing the traditional scarlet gowns of the University of St Andrews, given a charter in 1411, process casually from chapel, down the hill and out to the end. A pier has welcomed boats there since about 1100, but the first *stone* pier, a wide, tall wall in the sea, was constructed in the sixteenth century, in part with stones from the cathedral ruins.[4] The pier has since shielded the harbour from almost all of the arching, thunderous swells that occasionally barrel in from the North Sea. On the northern side of the pier is a series of parallel rock ledges, called skerries, which extend obliquely from the cliffs and are submerged at high tide, providing ideal caverns and nooks for invertebrates and fish. On the southern, protected side of the pier is a narrow channel out of the harbour. If you sail straight out and continue northeastwards, you will eventually arrive at the mountainous coast of Norway after a brief but seasickening voyage of some 350 miles.

From the tower you can see the university's Gatty Marine Laboratory, with its back to the harbour and its front facade facing the sea. William Carmichael McIntosh, an earnest biologist and writer about the local invertebrates and fisheries,

Claude Aubriet (c. 1665–1742), *European Lobster,* watercolour sketch. The current accepted scientific name is *Homarus gammarus.*

James Sowerby's illustration of *Palinurus vulgaris* (now *elephas*), the Common spiny lobster or crayfish, in William Elford Leach's *Malacostraca Podophthalmata Britanniæ ...* (1815). Leach, one of the leading crustacean biologists of his day, completed some of his early studies at the University of St Andrews.

founded this laboratory in 1896. On the other side of the pier, farther east along the coast and built into the cliffs, is the St Andrews Aquarium, which displays in tanks both a European spiny lobster and two resplendent royal blue specimens of *Homarus gammarus*.

The libraries of the University of St Andrews are visible from St Rule's Tower. Inside these stone buildings are stacks with brittle old manuscripts and volumes of history with odd lines, paragraphs and occasional articles on mankind's past relationship with the lobster. Also from the tower you can just see the slate-tiled roof of the building that houses the Bell Pettigrew Museum of Natural History. Here resides a giant pair of dusty old lobster claws and, preserved in jars of spirits, several pickled nineteenth-century lobsters collected from local Scottish waters or brought back from distant sailing voyages.

Tucked between all of this history and scholarship, perhaps in spite of it, is a tiny port at the base of the pier and the mouth of the Kinness Burn. St Andrews Harbour shelters a small fleet of fishermen, most of whom catch lobster and crab in the warmer months, just as men have done here for hundreds of years. The fishermen do not need to travel far to catch the European lobsters, which crawl around the rocks on the seaward side of the pier. The animals hide amidst the skerries and all around the dark bouldered coasts of St Andrews Bay and the rockweed edges of the Fife peninsula.

By the time Regulus arrived lobsters had been eating, moulting, copulating, releasing eggs and grazing their antennae on

Preserved specimens of various lobsters and freshwater crayfish, including two exceptionally large Norway lobsters, *Nephrops norvegicus* (bottom shelf, left of mounted *H. gammarus* claws), on display in the Bell Pettigrew Museum of Natural History, St Andrews. 19th-century Scottish naturalists collected several of these samples, which have served as teaching tools for generations of university students.

Upper Jurassic fossil of *Palinurina longipes* in lithographic limestone, Solenhofen, Bavaria, Germany.

the floor of the northern seas for tens of millions of years, looking almost exactly as we know them today while they watched (and ate) the evolutionary progression of a new group of animals we now know as cod, migrated around a few ice ages, and nibbled the remains of several drowned woolly mammoths.

Humans have been using shelled marine creatures for food or bait as long as our ancestors have been sitting heavy-browed around a campfire. Excavations of the Lussa Wood site on the island of Jura, on the west coast of Scotland, reveal the remnants of shelled oysters and mussels as early as 6500 BCE.[5] The Morton shell mound in Fife, a spear's throw from St Andrews, also dates back to the Stone Age. This midden was once a pile of some 10 million shells.[6] The Picts, at the time when Regulus allegedly arrived, surely ate a great deal of shellfish from the shores. Mussels, scallops, limpets and oysters could be picked directly off the rocks, while more mobile animals such as lobsters and crabs would have required a bit more skill: a chilly swim or a deft spear or hook. At the very least our ancestors

probably gathered large crustaceans stranded in tidal pools or washed up on the beach after a storm.

Archaeologists have not identified many lobster and crab remnants in early shell middens in the UK – or anywhere on earth really. Perhaps these animals weren't eaten in any great quantity, but more likely few records remain because the thin shells of crustaceans are more biodegradable: the exoskeletons haven't survived as well as did the more calcified shells of molluscs.[7] Only particularly hard parts of a lobster shell, such as the edges of large claws or the grinding mandibles, survive centuries of exposure or burial.[8] Perhaps sessile creatures and fish were so plentiful for ancient peoples that lobster was a smaller part of their diet. Maybe in some ecosystems vast fish populations kept lobster numbers down by gobbling their planktonic larvae, or ocean temperatures were such that lobsters didn't populate areas where they are now quite common. Yet archaeologists have, for example, excavated mandibular parts of the Cape rock lobster (*Jasus lalandii*) from Stone Age human rubbish in South Africa, as well as remnants of parts of the Red rock lobster (*Jasus edwardsii*) within Polynesian middens in New Zealand.[9]

When combining these rare archaeological finds with early depictions on artefacts and the accounts of European contacts with native peoples, we can rest assured that the gathering and eating of lobster or the use of lobster as bait or for other purposes was a part of pre-colonial coastal cultures on each and every populated continent and throughout the South Pacific and Caribbean. French explorer Nicolas Baudin, for example, observed during his visit to Tasmania in 1802:

> The oysters were of good quality, but the lobsters were far superior to those eaten in Europe by reason of the delicacy and lightness of their flesh. The natives appear to depend on these two creatures for their principal source

Lobster effigy, c. 1550 CE, clay and paint, Lamanai, Belize. Notice the human figure inside the mouth of this spiny lobster sculpture.

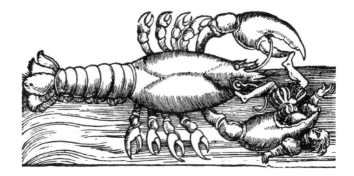

of food, for everywhere one finds piles of remains which indicate their heavy consumption of them.[10]

The earliest depiction of a lobster seems to be in a carving on a temple wall in Deir el-Bahri, Egypt, recording a voyage to the Red Sea in 1493 BCE.[11] The Peruvian Moche peoples created lobster motifs on ceramic vessels in the early centuries of the Common Era, and sources describe impressions of lobsters on early coins of the Mediterranean.[12]

The bold Abbot Regulus would have sailed from a part of the Roman-dominated world in the fourth century where this crustacean was well known. Craftsmen decorated the utensils of the Roman table with lobster designs. However, beyond Aristotle's excellent biological descriptions and a few artefacts, much of what remains on record about the human relationship to lobsters in ancient Greece and Rome, in the Middle Ages and into the Renaissance is difficult to substantiate and at times dubious. Charlemagne supposedly ate them nearly every night; he created legislation for regulating the lobster fishery that punished fishermen who brought rotten lobsters to market.[13]

Tiberius allegedly ordered the face of a fisherman who had offended him to be shredded with a spiny lobster's shell.[14] One yarn goes that a supper of stewed lobsters inspired one of Cicero's greatest speeches, and another spins that the Roman emperor Maximinus ate twenty lobsters at one seating. A nineteenth-century British professor wrote that 'one Pope is said to have hastened his death by their intemperate use'.[15]

In the first century Pliny the Elder wrote in a chapter on sea monsters about spiny lobsters in the Indian Ocean that were 'four cubits in length', the equivalent of 1.8 or 2.4 metres (6 or 8 feet).[16] Tales of leviathan lobsters have since persisted, perhaps in part due to Pliny's account, or maybe because they were indeed once much larger.

A fascination with giant individuals has been a significant part of our cultural relationship and interest in the lobster. Illustrations in sixteenth-century European natural histories by Albertus Magnus of Cologne, Olaus Magnus and Conrad Gesner depict man-eating lobsters capable of hauling sailors off their ships.[17] In the mid-eighteenth century Erich Pontoppidan wrote that off the coast of Norway fishermen reported lobsters that could spread their claws 2 metres (6 feet) wide and were 'so large and frightful' that no man was willing to attack them.[18]

Woodcut depicting North Sea leviathan lobsters in Olaus Magnus's *Historia de gentibus septentrionalibus* or *A Description of the Northern Peoples* (1555).

Though individuals of a few spiny lobster species can grow quite large, such as the Green rock lobster (*Jasus verreauxi*) found off the coasts of New Zealand and eastern Australia, the biggest and heaviest are the North Atlantic clawed lobsters, with the American lobster the largest on average.

To put some of the following in perspective, the majority of American lobsters caught and served today in restaurants weigh between 450 and 900 g (1–2 lb) alive, less than the weight of a small jar of pickles.

Europeans who sailed to North America in the seventeenth century wrote about exceptionally big bugs. They probably would not have recognized the American lobsters as a separate species, adding further to their surprise at their girth. William Wood and fellow Englishman John Josselyn both described twenty-pounders (9 kg) in separate accounts.[19] In 1630 Reverend Francis Higginson practically swore on his Bible in his narrative, assuring his readers back home that he was not exaggerating any of his observations. Relating only the truth 'without any frothy bumbasting words', Higginson wrote:

> And besides Basse wee take plentie of Scate and Thornbacks, and abundance of Lobsters, and the least Boy in

the Plantation [on Massachusetts Bay] may both catch and eat what he will of them. For my owne part I was soone cloyed [satiated] with them, they were so great, and fat, and luscious. I have seene some my selfe that have weighed 16 pound, but others have had divers [several] times so great Lobsters as have weighed 25 pound, as they assure mee.[20]

In 1911 the pre-eminent American lobsterologist, Francis Herrick, published his own investigations of claims about huge clawed lobsters. He confirmed several individuals over 9 kg (20 lb). The largest he endorsed at the time was a 15.5 kg (34 lb) lobster, whose carapace was 31 cm (12¼ inches) long and measured 52 cm (20½ inches) *around* the crusher claw.[21] A schooner off Sandy Hook, New Jersey, caught this male and brought it to Fulton Fish Market, making the *New York Times* on 20 March 1897 with the headline 'KING OF ALL THE LOBSTERS':

He measures nearly four feet and a half [1.4 m] in length from the tip of his formidable claws to the end of his tail. If he could stand erect he could clasp an ordinary man about the waist. His claws are strong and big enough to crush the wrist bones of a strong man . . . Estimating according to scientific rules of lobsters, the new acquisition is declared to be between thirty-eight and forty-five years old . . . He is the oldest and biggest lobster ever seen, and will be under scientific observation from now to the day of his death.[22]

Unfortunately, that day came within a week. This king lobster is still preserved, however, at the American Museum of Natural History.

Twentieth-century fishermen, with the ability to trawl nets in deep water, have dragged up a few American lobsters weighing over 18 kg (40 lb). The shell of a 19 kg (42 lb) specimen is mounted at the Museum of Science in Boston. According to the *Guinness Book of World Records* the largest lobster ever captured weighed 20.1 kg (44 lb 6 oz) and measured 107 cm (3 feet 6 inches) from tail to claw. This beast was netted off Nova Scotia in the winter of 1977 and met its demise at a seafood restaurant on Long Island.[23]

If you descend St Rule's Tower and walk away from the harbour, along cobbled old North Street and into the main library at the university, you can watch from the windows of the upper floors the lobster fishermen hauling their pots on the bay. The men motor out on most mid to low summer tides to tend their traps, called 'creels'. With usually one or two men per vessel they steer their boats tight along the coast, fishing at lower water so they can better see the rocks and place the creels.

Beginning to search through the stacks in the library, through the early narratives, you'll find that it was not only stories of gargantuan lobsters that intrigued travellers, but the animal's abundance and ease of capture. In 1521, the year before he became a lecturer at St Andrews, John Major described fishermen catching lobsters, which he called 'polypods', on the south side of the Firth of Forth. The townspeople did not even need bait:

> In Lent and in summer, at the winter and the summer solstice, people go in early morning from my own Gleg-hornie and the neighbouring parts to the shore, drag out the polypods and crabs with hooks, and return at noon with well-filled sacks. At these seasons the tide is at its lowest, and the polypods and crabs take shelter under the rocks by the sea. A hook is fastened to the end of a stick, and when the fish becomes aware of the wood or

A 25 lb (11.3 kg) American lobster caught in a trawl net off the coast of New England.

iron, it catches the same with one of its joints, thus connecting itself with the stick, which the fisherman then at once draws up.[24]

When European explorers arrived by ship at the coast of North America, they trusted lobster as a familiar food from home. In 1578 Anthonie Parckhurst wrote to encourage settlement in Newfoundland: 'No surely, but thus I doe: with three hookes stretched foorth in the ende of a pole . . . I may take up in lesse then halfe a day Lobsters sufficient to finde three hundred men for a dayes meate.'[25] A 1597 account of a voyage visiting Cape Breton Island found 'the greatest multitude of lobsters that ever we heard of'. The men caught over 140 lobsters with one haul of a 'little draw net'.[26] The chronicler of a 1607 expedition claimed that in shallow water off the coast of Nova Scotia they gaffed fifty 'great Lopsters' within an hour: 'Thear ar great store of them you may near Lad a Ship wth them. & they are of greatt bignesse I have nott Seen the Lyke in Ingland.'[27]

Writing about the mid-coast of present-day Maine, James Rosier described how his expedition caught enormous quantities of fish and 'very good and great Lobsters'.[28] A decade later John Smith wrote about the entirety of New England in 1616: 'You shall scarce finde any Baye, shallow shore, or Cove of land, where you may not take many Clampes [clams], or Lobsters, or both at your pleasure, and in many places lode your boat if you please.'[29] Thomas Morton in his *New English Canaan* (1637) described lobsters 'infinite in store in all the parts of the land'.[30] He explained that he grew bored of eating them after one day, using them instead for bait to catch bass.

Several explorers described how the Native Americans used lobster. Frenchman Marc Lescarbot wrote that the natives along the coasts of the Canadian Maritimes gathered large quantities of shellfish, including lobsters.[31] Native Americans invited Rosier's party to sit and smoke from a pipe made from the 'short claw' of a lobster, 'which will hold ten of our pipes full'.[32] Morton described the 'Salvages' gathering at the shore for several weeks to eat and dry lobsters for storage.[33] In 1634 William Wood wrote in *New England's Prospect*:

> In the summer these Indian women, when lobsters be in their plenty and prime, they dry them to keep for winter, erecting scaffolds in the hot sunshine, making fires likewise underneath them (by whose smoke the flies are expelled) till the substance remain hard and dry.[34]

Sailing to farther parts of the globe, European explorers wrote of the plentiful supply of spiny lobsters in the Southern Hemisphere. Several voyagers described the lobsters of the Juan Fernández Islands. This tiny archipelago off southern Chile became famous thanks to the marooning of Andrew Selkirk, a Scottish sailor raised on the south side of Fife. Selkirk's four-year trial was the inspiration for *Robinson Crusoe* (1719) and though Daniel Defoe chose not to describe his hero dining on the Juan Fernández crawfish or spiny lobster (*Jasus frontalis*), Selkirk surely did – or at least according to his rescuer, Captain Woodes Rogers, who wrote: 'Immediately our Pinnace return'd from the shore, and brought abundance of Craw-fish, with a Man cloth'd in Goat-Skins, who look'd wilder than the first Owners of them.'[35] John Howell, who wrote a biography of Selkirk, explained that the castaway often captured huge lobsters, then either broiled (grilled) or boiled them, seasoning with pimento. After his years on the island and the voyage home, Selkirk returned to Fife and some peaceful time as a gentleman lobsterman:

He purchased a boat for himself, and often, when the weather would permit, he made little excursions, but always alone; and day after day he spent in fishing, either in the beautiful bay of Largo or at Kingscraig Point, where he would loiter till evening among its romantic cliffs, catching lobsters, his favourite amusement, as they reminded him of the crawfish of Juan Fernandez.[36]

Lord George Anson, who visited Juan Fernández aboard the *Centurion* in the eighteenth century, wrote that the 'sea craw-fish' were likely the best in the world for their flavour, abundance, and size, weighing 'eight or nine pounds apiece' (3.6 or 4 kg).[37] There were so many spiny lobsters that their boat hooks speared them by accident when the men manouevred their launch on and off the shore. When the *HMS Collingwood* visited Juan Fernández, Lieutenant Frederick Walpole became intoxicated with lobster:

The bottom was literally lined with crawfish of a large size; some must have weighed five pounds [2.25 kg] at least . . . Catching crawfish was one of the favourite amusements of the seamen: one man held a pole, on which was fastened a bait, thrown into the water near the beach; one or two others stood ready, and when the crawfish, allured by the bait, had approached within attainable distance, these dogs of war pounced upon him . . . The boat-keepers in the boats alongside used to let down pieces of net spread on the hoop of a cask, with a piece of bait inside it: in a few minutes this was hauled up, and one of our simple friends generally appeared seated on it, greatly enjoying the travelling; sometimes two or three came up, struggling for standing-room. But enough of crawfish: I will only add,

that we thoroughly enjoyed both the catching and the eating. We had crawfish for breakfast, crawfish for dinner, crawfish for supper, and crawfish for any accidental meal we could cram in between.[38]

Explorers throughout other parts of the Pacific were similarly impressed with the numbers and taste of spiny lobsters. Sir Joseph Banks, for example, when off the coast of New Zealand with Captain Cook, wrote: 'But above all the luxuries we met with the lobsters or sea crawfish must not be forgot . . . Of them we bought great quantities of the natives every where to the Northward, who catch them by diving near the shore, feeling first with their feet till they find out where they lie.'[39] Nearly two centuries later archaeologist and adventurer Thor Heyerdahl described native women catching spiny lobsters this same way, at night, from the shore of Easter Island.[40]

Joseph Lycett, *Aborigines spearing fish, others diving for crayfish, a party seated beside a fire cooking fish, c.* 1817, watercolour leaf in an album. This depiction of people catching crayfish suggests lobster was a part of native diets in New South Wales before European contact.

Despite the large size and surprising plenty reported in so many of these narratives, Europeans never developed either the skill or the taste to dry lobster or smoke the meat. Lobsters can survive for hours without water. I've biked home after fishing on several hot afternoons with a few bugs in a plastic bag, and they were just as active when I went to cook them several hours later. Lobsters can survive days when packed in something cool and damp, but they degrade rapidly once killed or cooked. They die quickly in fresh water. Either picked or whole, the flesh doesn't hold up to salting, so early explorers and settlers never developed lobstering as a commercial venture despite their abundance. Colonists thought of them primarily as a useful local supply of fresh food or a convenient source for bait to catch fish that *could* be salted and shipped.

Sketch of a Maori bartering a spiny lobster for a handkerchief from Sir Joseph Banks, 1769. Scholars believe this to be drawn by a native Polynesian priest named Tupaia who sailed aboard the *Endeavour* with Banks and Captain James Cook.

Adriaen van Utrecht's 1644 oil of a *Festive Meal*. Dutch and other European painters regularly included lobsters in their still lifes, surely for the splash of red as much as the intimation of wealth and sexuality. The lobster's widespread appearance in these paintings provides rough clues for environmental historians; evidently *Homarus gammarus* was fished and available at the market.

The first substantial lobster industry seems to have originated in Norway in the seventeenth century, arising to supply the demand for lobsters in Holland, which had exhausted its own stocks. According to nineteenth-century biologist and historian Axel Boeck, Norwegians knew of lobsters for centuries – they appear briefly in the poetic lines of their sagas – but the country's citizens, even fishermen, had little taste for them at the table. It was not until the Dutch sailed across the North Sea to search foreign waters for lobsters that a Norwegian commercial fishery began. Boeck writes that by 1674 the port of Flekkefjord 'was visited by ten lobster-ships', and from this starting point various other harbours grew quickly into lobster ports around the south coast of Norway.[41] Merchants shipped the live lobsters in seawater compartments, 'wells', or packed them in boxes with seaweed. The Dutch sent gifts to the clergy of these ports in the form of cheese and cakes, hoping they would encourage the locals to catch and sell them lobster. Boeck reports: 'This succeeded so well near Lister that I find that a man on July 7, 1699, had his ground solemnly consecrated so as to prevent other people from catching lobsters there.'[42] When the clergy was no longer relevant, traders gave the fishermen clay pipes and provided twine to tie up the lobsters' claws during shipment.

Boeck writes that by the eighteenth century Norwegian lobster ports received Dutch ships at least twice a year, in late autumn and early spring. Norwegian lobstermen organized to raise their price, then began to bicker in court over valuable lobstering territories, which ended in a decree in 1728 that lobster fishing was free and open to all. The Norwegian ports expanded to serve a growing demand from English merchants who had been supplementing their own domestic catches by importing tens of thousands of lobsters from places such as the islands of Helgoland off Germany. In 1733 alone Norwegians waved farewell to 23 shipments sailing for Holland, a total of 160,000 lobsters, as well as 41 apparently smaller cargoes bound for England.[43]

Though signs of depletion along the Norwegian coasts had been observed some seventy years earlier, with officials urging conservation, Norway still exported nearly 350,000 lobsters between 1804 and 1806, according to Boeck. The historic Norwegian lobster industry peaked in 1827 and 1828, when merchants sent from a wide variety of ports some 1.5 million lobsters each year to Holland and across the North Sea to Britain. The fishery then dipped for over a generation as conservation laws were finally put in place and enforced. By the 1860s exports were back at a new high. [44] When Boeck completed his account of the Norwegian lobster fishery in 1869, fishmongers at Billingsgate Market in London sold hundreds of thousands of lobsters a year from Norway, stacking them alongside bugs fetched up from around the British Isles. That same year M.

Schele de Vere wrote that a visitor to Billingsgate would see 'pyramids of lobsters, a vast moving mass of spiteful claws and restless feelers, savage at being torn from their clear, cool homes in Norwegian waters'.[45]

Historian James Coull wrote that demand for lobster was so high in London from the late eighteenth century that the market 'was almost insatiable'.[46] Responding to the depletion of more traditional food fisheries, the cod and herring, Scottish fishermen from ports such as St Andrews gradually began to pursue lobsters with greater attention, whereas previously the catching of these crustaceans was only an occasional practice. The fishermen sent the lobsters to London by sail, then steam, then rail, in vessels with flow-through wells to keep the lobsters alive or in boxes packed with seaweed.[47]

St Andrews was a much busier harbour in earlier centuries, supporting a larger fleet with dozens of vessels bound beyond

Two lobstermen in a wooden boat piled with lobster traps off the Norwegian coast, 1934, working in a similar way to how men have fished these waters for hundreds of years.

The Fish Merchant, an 18th-century canvas sometimes ascribed to Hogarth, but probably by Joseph van Aken (d. 1739); a fishmonger displays both a clawed and spiny lobster on his counter.

Telfer Thomson from Buckhaven, Fife, dressed for fishing and holding a creel for lobsters and crabs, 1900. The men crafted these traps from branches, typically ash, and made the netting by hand.

the stone pier for international trade or sailing out to net herring, sprat or groundfish. The commercial lobster fishery started in St Andrews in the early 1800s and has remained steady and profitable, but it has never been more than a small affair compared to larger lobster fisheries in the Orkney Islands and the western coast of Scotland, or even the more productive ports around Fife such as Crail or Anstruther. As William McIntosh predicted, in the twentieth century the most valuable commercial crustacean in the area was actually the Norway lobster, or scampi, a much smaller clawed lobster caught with nets beyond St Andrews Bay.

Our man Francis Herrick made a voyage to St Andrews in 1896, probably in part to see the Gatty Marine Laboratory and visit with Professor McIntosh, who shared his concern about the depletion of *Homarus* species. Herrick wrote of the fishermen's traps:

72

Men working on creels beside the famous pier of St Andrews Harbour, 1908.

Those examined . . . were small cylinders, made of a wooden frame covered with netting, and were anchored by means of a flat stone tied to the bottom. A fisherman with whom I conversed on the beach had 40 of these creels, and was going to haul them at 5 o'clock that evening, but with no expectation of taking any lobsters, for, as he expressed it, the sea was too calm; rough weather brought better luck.[48]

If you stroll down to St Andrews Harbour today, you'll find the Gatty laboratories still buzzing with activity, although they have long since sold their research boat, the *rv Homarus*. Closer to the pier the majority of the fishermen's craft fly the flag of Scotland off their stern, the white cross of St Andrews on a blue field. These creel boats are squat, constructed of wood and fibreglass, and are generally between 6 and 9 metres (20 and 30 feet) long, although I've seen one man still lobstering with a rowing boat.

The fishermen's traps, small by international standards, are hemispheric in shape and built with plastic frames and plastic-coated mesh. The men fish from 300 to 800 traps per boat. They mark the whereabouts of their creels with lines attached to buoys that are fashioned out of brightly coloured plastic detergent bottles and sometimes a flag on a pole. They almost always use frozen bait, because that's what is available. The St Andrews fishermen sell their catch to wholesalers in town. If the wholesalers don't sell it to local fishmongers or to the fancy local restaurants that serve the wealthy golfers, they load the animals in a lorry bound for Edinburgh or across to Glasgow or maybe on a train down to London. In 2010 some thirty men were involved in the St Andrews lobster and crab fishery, mostly older chaps, and nearly every one of them had at least one other job, storing their boats on the dock during the dark, gale-filled winter.[49]

None of these fishermen can afford to stay in the quaint mediaeval homes up the hill or beside the harbour, even though these were once the tiny, draughty stone shacks of their grandfathers and great grandfathers, fishermen who told stories of huge, plentiful, 'muckle' lobsters.

4 Building a Better Lobster Trap

The lobsters catch themselves, for they cling to the netting
on which the bait is placed of their own accord, and thus are
drawn up. They sell them for two cents apiece. Man needs
to know but little more than a lobster in order to catch them
in his traps.

Henry David Thoreau, 1865 [1]

John Whittaker's lobsterboat *Whistler* smells of fishy labour,
but it is not rank unless a bait barrel is left open, attracting both
flies and gulls. *Whistler* is 13 metres (42 feet) long and has the
classic lines of a New England lobsterboat: a high, proud bow
to cut through the seas, a covered house forward, then a rail
that smooths aft into a low, wide stern that adds stability and is
easier for working the traps. The boat is fitted with radar to find
the way in the fog and with a modest array of electronics to help
find his gear. Whittaker can steer from inside or from the open
area beside the port rail, from where he hauls the traps. He brings
these pots to the surface by hooking a buoy with a gaff, leading
the attached line through a pulley on a davit, and then inboard
around a spinning hydraulic drum. Banging hundreds of pots
each day against the port side of the hull has rendered it scratched
and scarred, like the skin of an old warrior seal.

Securing a lobster, like catching a mouse, is a simple matter in
concept but not always so in practice. Historically, people throughout the world waded into shallow waters for lobsters, hitching
them with gaffs, poles and spears. They tangled lobsters in nets,
nabbed them with snares or free-dived and snatched the lobsters
out of their dens. [2] All sorts of commercial and recreational fishermen searching for clawed, spiny and slipper lobsters – from
Norway to Namibia, from Belize to Bangladesh – have tried at its

With a few traps stacked on the stern, *Whistler* steams out of Noank, Connecticut, bound for Whittaker's fishing grounds in Long Island Sound.

plainest to attract these crustaceans, pull them undamaged to the surface and then have a method to bring the lobsters ashore and preserved for the consumer's kitchen. In recent times, almost wherever you are, catching a lobster is rife with complications and intricacies. As a commercial or even a recreational endeavour it usually requires a significant financial investment, an understanding of government regulations and an enormous and varied store of knowledge, experience and good fortune.

Even in the same general location fishermen often employ a few different strategies to catch a lobster. Around the coasts of Ireland and England, for example, fishermen have been catching clawed and spiny lobsters by traps, diving, and thin-meshed nets. In the waters of Hawaii Euell Gibbons described his experience as a commercial and recreational catcher of spiny lobster. He caught these animals with traps, with nets at times 1,000 feet long, and even with a fishing pole with a three-pronged hook and a piece of bait. Gibbons wrote:

> All these ways of catching Spiny Lobsters are fun, but the way to wring the maximum amount of sport from this

creature is to dive down to the bottom and catch it with nothing but your hands . . . Wear a pair of heavy gloves . . . You may carry a spear, but use it only on those that are in holes too deep for you to reach them. When you get a Spiny Lobster in your hands, hold on for dear life. It will flap that strong tail mightily, and set up a terrible commotion, and the first time this happens most neophyte divers panic and let go. It is all bluff, and you can soon have your Spiny Lobster safely into a bag if you just hold on.[3]

With the popularization of scuba diving, beginning in the 1950s, people began collecting underwater animals more easily and in deeper waters, rendering lobsters, as Gibbons put it, 'at your mercy'. Diving for lobsters has since been regulated on several coasts. In southern California, for example, a diving recreational fisherman is restricted to a certain number of legal-sized lobsters per day, scuba gear isn't allowed in all areas, and a person may only dive during a specified season and only with hands – no spears or other tools. The Kuna Indians of Panama's San Blas region have outlawed scuba diving for the commercial

A wooden tool for catching crustaceans, carved by the Yahgan peoples of Tierra del Fuego.

catch of their spiny lobsters (*Panulirus sp.*), allowing only free-diving with masks, flippers and snares from canoes during daylight hours.[4] The regulations for the Galápagos Islands aren't quite as strict, as they allow diving for spiny and slipper lobsters (*Panulirus penicillatus* and *P. gracilis, Scyllarides astori*) from a small boat, usually at night, with the aid of hoses pumped with compressed air, a 'hookah' system.[5] In Australia and Papua New Guinea lobstermen use a similar hookah method in the Torres Strait; they also free-dive for their Ornate spiny lobster (*P. ornatus*), as do men in Thailand and the Philippines.[6]

If you don't want to get wet, a popular early lobstering device used into the nineteenth century in Britain and consequently in North America was the hoop net: a netted pouch woven onto a cylindrical wood or metal ring, often made from a barrel hoop, with bait suspended over the top. The hoop net required tending from a rowing boat, and a fisherman had to pull up the line at the right time, before the lobsters crawled elsewhere.[7] Recreational fishermen still occasionally use hoop nets today, often from a kayak.

In the early Norwegian lobster fishery men used tongs that measured about 3.5 metres (12 feet) long, which they wielded over the side of a boat in the same way oyster tongs were once used. Some Norwegian lobstermen used lobster tongs into the nineteenth century but the Dutch, encouraging them to catch lobster more efficiently and not damage the animals with the tongs' tines, introduced as early as 1717 a basket-style trap to the Norwegian coast. The Dutch seem to have adapted the idea from their eel trap.[8] It remains difficult to say, however, which culture *first* invented the transportable trap intended primarily for lobsters – one that allows a fisherman to leave it and return some hours or days later to retrieve his or her loot. This type of trap enables a lobsterman to fish deeper waters and set more pots.

Traps remain the most common lobstering tool around the world. Numerous types, assembled in a variety of shapes and sizes, have been used and deployed in all oceans, for dozens of species of lobster. Fishermen along the coasts of Japan, India, South Africa, Hawaii and the Canary Islands all use different styles of lobster traps, yet all the pots serve in roughly the same way. British fisherman-author Alan Spence, writing about the different traps around Britain such as the 'inkwell' design of the English Channel versus the French 'barrel-style', explained: 'Each community likes to think that their design is superior to all others in catching and holding qualities.'[9] Some variations are better suited to local conditions and supplies, while others are simply regional, traditional constructions, no more effective than any other. Fishermen first built their traps with materials such as wood, bamboo, willow, wicker, leather and natural fibre netting, but now most are made with at least some metal or plastic. Nearly all types of traps have a funnelled entrance, which serves as a type of one-way valve, designed so lobsters cannot climb back out after they've been enticed inside by some sort of bait.

A lobsterman flings an inkwell-style lobster trap over the rail, just off the coast of Inishmore, one of the Aran islands off the Atlantic coast of Ireland.

John Whittaker's lobster pots, like those throughout New England and Canada, are built of vinyl-coated wire, are rectangular and are larger than most dormitory refrigerators. Even before anything is caught inside or growing on the frame, Whittaker's traps are back-breakers, each weighing 29–32 kg (65–70 lb). In part this is because every pot is fixed with several bricks or a slab of cement so it will sink quickly, land correctly and stay put against powerful currents, even when dropped as far as 107 metres (350 feet) below the surface.[10] Each trap has a door at the top to allow access for hanging bait and removing, 'picking', the lobsters, and two compartments. One, called 'the kitchen', has two netted funnel heads for the lobsters to enter as they hunt for the bait hung in the middle of the trap. After snacking in the kitchen, the lobster then crawls through an internal funnel that is presumably easier to navigate than the ones it used to enter, but this funnel leads into a second compartment, 'the parlour', in which the lobster cannot seem to go anywhere.

From an environmentalist perspective lobster traps are much better for ocean ecosystems than trawl, trammel or tangle nets. Pots have minimal by-catch and they do much less damage to the sea bottom since they remain relatively stationary. Wooden traps – still used in many parts of the world – cost more these days to make and maintain and are subject to rot and marine fouling. This degradability is a positive feature if you're a lobster. If a fisherman loses a trap on the bottom, perhaps due to a storm or the cutting of the buoy line by a propeller, a wooden pot will eventually break up. Plastic or metal gear, on the other hand, takes longer to decompose and can continue catching lobsters for years, known as 'ghost fishing'. Lobsters can survive quite a while in a trap. They can eat plankton or dine on other captured creatures – a crab, a fish, an eel, another lobster – or find sustenance from the thick fouling community that often

A wooden trap on the ocean bottom, illustrating W. H. Bishop's *The Lobster at Home in Maine Waters* (1881).

THE LOBSTER AT HOME.

In the spring, the lobster, who has passed the winter months in deep water, returns again inshore. He has found the deep water both tranquil and warm, while the shallower expanses near land have been troubled to the bottom by furious gales and chilled by the drifting ice. Thirty fathoms is a very fair depth for his winter home, while in summer the trap in which he is generally captured gathers in a goodly number if sunk in a depth of five fathoms, or even less. A few lobsters burrow in the mud and in a manner hibernate, but forms on the pot itself. Depending on the coast and the nature of the bottom, traps regularly arrive on the boat's rail with little jungles of algae, barnacles, mussels, sponges, sea squirts, skeleton shrimp, crabs and sea stars. And even if a lobster starves to death in the pot, it might serve as bait for other animals – so this ghost trap business can be an unseen cyclical problem.

To avoid ghost traps, laws in several lobster fisheries require a removable 'escape vent' fixed with biodegradable metal clips. If the pot is lost on the ocean bottom, this vent will eventually break off and the lobsters can climb out. Some regulations require that the vent has a plastic opening of a specified width, allowing smaller lobsters that are not close to legal size to swim free.

Though wire traps stack more easily, last longer and are cheaper to make and repair, their use, first developed for the offshore lobster fishery, has not come without a certain reluctance. Like most new fishing technologies, especially sonar and the hydraulic trap hauler, the wire pot is one more convenience that encourages more people to go out and lobster. Vivian Volovar, author of her own children's book, *Lobster Lady* (2007), has been fishing for bugs almost as long as Whittaker. Volovar said:

> Most of these fishermen, they can't fish now without all the electronics, they can't tell what the wind's doing or what's going on . . . They got all the brand new wire gear because they got something else supporting them . . . Can you knit funnels? No. If they couldn't buy everything they had, they couldn't fish. They don't know how to build pots or do any of this stuff. They got into the business because they had a lot of money behind them. And a good credit card.[11]

The majority of lobstermen fish in fairly shallow water and close to the coast, but a few lobster fisheries seek the animals in

An offshore lobsterboat out of Point Judith, Rhode Island, 1997. Barrels on deck overflow with dead skate, a common bait-fish, to be hung inside the industrial-sized wire traps stacked behind the deck-house.

deeper seas. The North American offshore lobster fishery peaked in the 1970s, but a small number of boats still lobster hundreds of miles from land. They fish more traps on a string and use larger boats that require more industrial gear. One offshore lobsterboat in 2008, for example, fished over 240 km (150 miles) off the coast of New Jersey in approximately 150 metres (500 feet) of water. The crew hauled strings of 50 pots, each weighing some 45 kg (100 lb). They were out for a week at a time.[12] Large fishing vessels engaged in the spiny lobster fishery (*Palinurus gilchristi*) off South Africa can carry some 2,000 plastic traps aboard and set strings of 100–200 pots on one string, sinking them as deep as 200 metres (650 feet). A few of these vessels have the technology to freeze the tails immediately on board.[13]

The faster and bigger boats, the improved navigation systems, the wire traps, the synthetic ropes, the powered pot-haulers – it all just means that lobstermen can fish more gear, more often, in deeper water and in most weathers. More lobsters are being caught globally and there are more traps on the bottom trying to capture those that are left. Several lobster fisheries have experienced booms and busts, as seen in Brazil (*Panulirus argus* and *P. laevicauda*) and India (e.g. *Thenus orientalis*), which both saw prolific years in the second half of the twentieth century, fluctuations and then a steady decline, from which the stocks remain tenuous.[14] On many coasts, such as in the Galápagos, when spiny lobster populations were overfished, men went after the less profitable slipper lobsters.[15] Fishing practices have had an effect. Throughout Europe and the Mediterranean, for example, the use of thin-meshed nets beginning in the 1960s put a huge strain on the spiny lobster populations.[16]

In the 1960s the South Africa deep water lobster fishery boomed, with occasional 'jackpot hauls' of the Natal spiny lobster, *Palinurus delagoae*. Today, the fleet and catch are a fraction of what they were.

ANY LOBSTER MEASURING LESS THAN EIGHT INCHES FROM THE TIP OF THE BEAK TO THE END OF THE TAIL WHEN SPREAD OUT FLAT TO BE RETURNED

Government managers have used a variety of tools to regulate regional lobster industries. It can be slightly easier than other fisheries since crustaceans are less mobile but, at the same time, the variety and length of highly transient larval stages make predicting stock sizes a challenge. There is never enough ecological information to make confident management decisions, especially with lesser known spiny and slipper species.

Several lobster fisheries limit the number of commercial or recreational traps per person, and some have limited the number of people that can be involved at all. A few countries have lobstering seasons, such as Spain, Greece, Australia and Canada. One management strategy, recently put in place by Brazil in an effort to keep track of its fleet of 800 or so lobster-boats, requires that every vessel be equipped with a satellite monitoring system.[17] A strategy enforced in most spiny fisheries, as in Western Australia, is a scientifically determined annual quota that the collective fishermen in a given area may not exceed. This total allowable catch can keep prices in check while maintaining stocks.

One of the most common management tools used in nearly all lobster fisheries is the mandate to refrain from harvesting female lobsters with eggs visible under the abdomen, known as 'eggers' or 'berried', or even to gather 'brood-stock' female lobsters that have been recently identified with eggs. To identify the latter, fishermen and managers in some countries cut a 'v-notch'

Scottish fisherman's gauge to determine the legal size of a lobster that may be brought to shore. Lobster was measured from the beak, or rostrum, to the end of the tail. Engraved on the other side is 'IV. Lobster Act 1877'.

in the tail-fin before they return an egger into the water so as to notify the next lobstermen. A v-notch can last for a couple of moults after a female has laid her eggs. Regulations in nearly all lobster fisheries declare a minimum size bug that can be brought ashore, usually measured by the length of the carapace. Managers sometimes set a maximum size as well to protect the most prolific breeders (while also helping the live-market dealers who have difficulty selling larger individuals to restaurants). Given these restrictions, most trap lobstermen spend the majority of their time *throwing back* lobsters, usually hoping for just a few keepers per pot.

After a lobsterman has learned the local regulations, he or she needs at least some understanding of economics. Lobster is a luxury commodity. The price a lobsterman gets for a catch is often out of his or her control and not even necessarily based on the health of the local population. Within the basic tenets of supply and demand a lobsterman is dependent on the consumer's willingness to go out for a fancy meal – and lobster markets and products are expanding to literally all corners of the earth.

Because of the price fetched for a single animal and its coastal habitat, lobstering is one of the few commercial fisheries remaining that can be viable for one or two people. John Whittaker, for example, is a single owner-operator. This makes him vulnerable to the cost of fuel and the price the draggers set for catching the majority of his bait. These bait-catching men, in turn, are also dependent on fuel costs, as well as immensely strict limitations for conservation purposes. Once Whittaker has caught the lobsters, he sells to a wholesaler, a fish market or directly to a restaurant. He does not have access to winter storage facilities, known as lobster pounds, to keep the animals alive to wait for better prices, as they do on a large industrial scale in

Canada. Whittaker also has no local cooperative that he might join, which can help cut costs and negotiate collectively, a technique employed by fishermen in other parts of the US and Mexico. Meanwhile, to make matters still more competitive for Whittaker, the supermarket just a few miles from his dock offers frozen spiny lobster tails from Nicaragua and South Africa. Across the aisle gurgle live clawed lobsters in a tank with claw bands that say 'Canada Wild'.

Beyond fishing technology, government regulations and the fluctuations of global trade, the lobsterman is also subject to small- and large-scale environmental factors beyond his or her control. In Whittaker's Long Island Sound the health and productivity of the lobster population has diminished due to several factors: large-scale die-offs to the west, an oil spill to the east, various types of industrial and coastal pollution, rising water temperature and a significant intraspecies shell disease. Somehow he has held on to his business, largely due to his experience, skill and hard work. Yet on the morning of 11 June 2010 he picked up his local newspaper before going aboard *Whistler* and read this headline: 'Regulators weigh five-year lobstering ban in southern New England'.[18]

Several of the global commercial lobster stocks, like all the world's fisheries, are in some level of decline. Diseases, viruses, overfishing, human pollution and climate change all threaten once vibrant lobster stocks in every ocean. A few lobster species are especially threatened regionally, such as the spiny lobster off the coast of South Africa and Namibia (*Jasus lalandii*), the spiny lobster off Taiwan (*Panulirus japonicus*) and the European lobster off the coast of Turkey.[19] As of now, however, no commercial lobster species is on the endangered species list, although, in truth, it is difficult for invertebrates to get that sort of status. In 2009 a group of international experts met in Taiwan to determine if any lobsters deserved to be listed on the International Union for Conservation of Nature's 'Red List Index'. British zoologist Nadia Dewhurst wrote:

> Preliminary results from the workshop indicate that a low proportion of the world's lobster species [they count about 250] are threatened with extinction. However, over 40% of species have been preliminarily placed in the Data Deficient category, of which 80% are known from the Indo-Pacific region particularly around Japan, Taiwan, China, the Philippines, and Indonesia . . . The results do however highlight that lobster fisheries are in fact some of the best managed fisheries: all of the major commercial species . . . were assessed as Least Concern.[20]

The group pointed out that many lobster species have wide geographical ranges, which has helped their status, regardless of regional depletions. They felt that 'poor fisheries management' has led to their concern for the health of populations such as the Caribbean spiny lobster, the Juan Fernández spiny lobster, and the St Paul spiny lobster (*Jasus paulensis*).[21]

Meanwhile, a surprising and inexplicable success story has emerged with the American lobster in the Gulf of Maine, just a few hundred miles to the east of Whittaker's Long Island Sound. These lobstermen are catching the same species but doing immensely better. *Homarus americanus* remains the lobster of highest international value and tonnage caught. Fishermen haul out of the sea tens of thousands of tonnes more of these bugs each year than those of any other lobster fishery on earth, employing some 40,000 commercial lobstermen and thousands more in shoreside industries.[22] In 2004 The Lobster Institute estimated the economic impact of this fishery to be from US$2.4 to

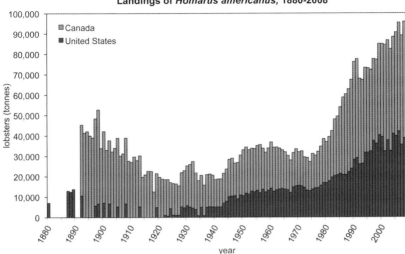

Landings of *Homarus americanus*, 1880-2008

Landings of *Homarus americanus* in tonnes, 1880–2008. Several data points are missing for the US before 1950, and US landings before then include only those from the major lobster fisheries states, from Connecticut to Maine.

4 billion.[23] This craggy stretch of coastline, with its endless coves and islands, extends from about the Isle of Shoals eastward and northward, up around Nova Scotia, New Brunswick and Prince Edward Island. On a much larger scale than anywhere else in the world the communities around the Gulf of Maine are dependent economically and even culturally on the harvest of lobster. Thankfully for them, despite highly intense fishing effort over the last half-century, this lobster population has remained seemingly vigorous. Many believe that it is one of the few healthy wild fisheries – of any marine species – left on our planet.

So why has this *Homarus americanus* fishery in the Gulf of Maine and the Canadian Maritimes fared so well? As with all fisheries questions, the answer is complicated and requires a look backward.

Commercial lobster fishing along these coasts actually did not get going until the mid-nineteenth century, primarily because of the challenges of shipping live product. Early settlers perceived abundant lobsters more as a local food source, as livestock feed, crop fertilizer or bait. During the eighteenth century, when the rebellious colonists were calling the red-coated British soldiers 'lobsters' and their ships 'lobster boxes', the fishermen in the regions of Massachusetts, Rhode Island and New York delivered live bugs in well boats to the urban centres of New York City and Boston. When these men could not meet the public demand, often because of overfishing, they sailed farther east, into the cold, productive, unspoiled waters of Maine. Here they set their traps, beginning around the 1820s.[24] Just like the Norwegians toward the Dutch, the fishermen in Maine soon realized they could do the lobstering themselves, so they restricted this fishing to Mainers and began sailing their own vessels to deliver *their* bugs to the cities.

When canning technology, first invented and perfected in France and Scotland, arrived to the region in the 1840s, the game changed completely. Here was a shipment and preservation solution, able to expand both market and demand. Historians Martin and Lipfert point out: 'It is a measure of *Homarus*

H. W. Elliott and Capt. J. W. Collins, 'Lobster fishing-boats of Bristol, Maine', 1887. This type of craft, known as a smack, often had flow-through wells to enable it to travel significant distances or several days to market with the lobsters kept alive.

W. K. Lewis, c. 1860s, made his fortune canning lobsters and other foods, beginning with his first factory on Isle au Haut, Maine. By 1883 the firm of W. K. Lewis & Brothers owned fifteen canneries in Maine and the Maritimes.

americanus's reputation among gourmets that it was one of the first items canned commercially in the United States.'[25] The Lobster Rush was on.

Canning overtook the live market and dozens of canneries sprouted up along the coast. By 1880 there were 23 active canneries in the state of Maine, the majority built exclusively for lobster.[26] Steamships carried about half of the canned Maine lobster and nearly all of the Canadian meat back to Europe, whose own lobster fisheries were much smaller due to oceanographic limitations and the fatigue of centuries of human impact.[27]

The Canadians were a bit slower to capitalize on the international value of lobster, but the fishery moved inevitably eastward. The lobster stocks around their coastline, according to a major government report, 'need only be restricted by the demand, for the supply is almost unlimited'.[28] In 1881 an English visitor named John Rowan observed with amazement that 'lobster spearing' was a sport in Halifax and that little boys collected hundreds with hooks and sticks off the shore. Rowan described farmers in New Brunswick fertilizing acres of potato fields with lobsters gathered from the beach after a gale. He wrote: 'To give some idea of the little value put upon lobsters by the country people, I may mention that on some parts of the coast they boil them for their pigs, but are ashamed to be seen eating lobsters themselves. Lobster shells about a house are looked upon as signs of poverty and degradation.'[29] There

and I supposed all dec
hum by that time, or ou[
The smack nowaday
the wharf of the lobst(
the land side, the first

BOILING-ROOM.

'Boiling-room' in a lobster cannery, illustrating W. H. Bishop's 1881 *The Lobster at Home in Maine Waters.*

are accounts that fishermen bound for groundfish off the Grand Banks loaded their hold with lobsters to chop into pieces and stick on their hooks.[30] Rowan anticipated that the Canadian lobster would be a high value export: 'Is it unreasonable to expect that sooner or later some ingenious persons will turn these Nova Scotian lobsters into British gold?'[31]

The lobster canning industry spread further into Atlantic Canada. According to Farley Mowat, in 1873 there was one factory all the way north in Newfoundland. Just fifteen years later 26 small canneries were boiling along, contracting over 1,000 fishermen and filling some 3 million 1 lb (450 g) cans of *picked* meat.[32] Canneries used only the claws and tails, tossing or composting the remains. In 1881 W. H. Bishop observed at a cannery: 'The scarlet hue is seen in all quarters – on the steaming stretcher, in the great heaps on the tables, in scattered individuals on the floor, in a large pile of shells and refuse seen through the open door, and in an ox-cart-load of the same refuse, farther off, which is being taken away for use as a fertilizer.'[33]

The Lobster Rush around the Gulfs of Maine and St Lawrence reached its peak in the late nineteenth century. Canadians averaged over 41 million kg (90 million lb) of lobster landed annually in the late 1890s, a harvest bonanza that they would not achieve again for nearly a century.[34] As more men had been entering the business full-time, lobstering required more traps and more effort to gather continually smaller and smaller lobsters to fill the tins.

It is worth emphasizing here, however, that this nineteenth-century depletion of American lobster stocks, as had occurred earlier in northern Europe with *Homarus gammarus*, seems to be a result of intense effort and lack of regulation, *not* advanced technology. The regular use of the internal combustion engine and even the motorized trap hauler was still decades away.

A pile of lobsters at the Lewis cannery, Isle au Haut, *c.* 1870.

Meanwhile concern for the lobster population consistently grew louder during the Lobster Rush, as voiced in two major, separate reports by the Canadians and the Americans in 1873 and 1887.[35] As European countries had done, American states and the Canadians began to pass a series of conservation laws, but they were not easily regulated or nearly effective enough. In 1905 naturalist Alfred Goldsborough Mayer admonished:

'Unless wise laws are soon enforced for their protection the ruthless persecution to which the lobsters have been subjected will practically exterminate them, in so far as commerce is concerned.'[36] More humorously and perhaps indicative of public concern, Holman F. Day published a poem in 1900 titled 'Good-by Lobster', which ends with this verse:

I see, and sigh in seeing, in some distant, future age
Your varnished shell reposing under glass upon a stage,
The while some pundit lectures on the curios of the past,
And dainty ladies shudder as they gaze on you aghast.
And all the folks that listen will wonder vaguely at
The fact that once lived heathen who could eat a Thing
    like that.
Ah, that's the fate you're facing – but laments are all in
    vain
– Tell the dodo that you saw us when you lived down here
    in Maine.[37]

In 1915 our lobster expert Francis Herrick stood before the committee on fisheries in the Maine state legislature. He sounded the alarm of still worse times to come and argued for a maximum size limit to protect large females and all the eggs they produce. Herrick declared: 'The conservation of the lobster fishery is a purely economic problem, and if we strive to solve it upon the grounds of political bias or personal gain, we shall assuredly fail.'[38]

At least in terms of recorded landings, lobster populations in North America stabilized as regulations were added and enforced, but did not approach the tonnage of the nineteenth century. It was not until the 1940s that lobster landings increased significantly again, then absolutely exploded in the late 1980s.

No one knows the exact cause for this unprecedented rise, seen in no other lobster fishery – or barely *any* fishery – but theories abound. Anne Hayden and Philip Conkling, frequent writers on the marine policy of the area, wrote: 'There's a saying in the region: ask two lobstermen why there are so many lobsters in [Penobscot Bay], and you get three different answers.'[39] The same could be said for biologists. And policy makers.

Hayden co-authors a column for *National Fisherman* and has been involved in local fisheries issues for over twenty years. She told me: 'I've been accused of being obsessed with lobsters. But mostly by my family who are sick of hearing about them – though not sick of eating them for dinner.'[40] Hayden explains that landings do not always indicate the health of a population, but there are a variety of theories beyond an increase of effort as to why the lobster catches have skyrocketed in the Gulf of Maine. Predation by groundfish, such as cod and haddock, decreased due to overfishing of those species. In some areas a vigorous urchin fishery, fuelled by Japanese demand, cleared the sea floor of these herbivores, allowing an increased growth of coastal seaweeds, which gave more safe habitat for moulting lobsters. Subtle changes in water temperature and currents might have favoured reproduction. There may be an 'aquaculture effect', in which there are simply so many lobster traps in the water that the lobsters are actually being raised and fed until they get to legal size. In addition the coast of Maine and the Maritimes, in contrast to that of Long Island Sound and parts of Europe, has been less developed by industry and residential construction. Their waters are cleaner. Yet none of these arguments alone can explain it all. Hayden says that even the biological premise for shaping policy – the most basic logic that the more eggs there are in the water, the more lobsters there will be – doesn't receive much credence any more.[41]

Conservation and enforcement measures put in place seem to have helped, but state officials and the Coast Guard are unable to patrol every harbour and cannot, for example, make sure every fisherman isn't picking the meat from 'shorts' or scrubbing the eggs off legal-sized females. What seems to be different in Maine, for example, in comparison to the lobster industry in Long Island Sound or that of Brazil, has been voiced by anthropologist and economist Jim Acheson, who writes that regulations have not only been accepted and formed by local lobstermen, they are *enforced* by them. This lobster fishery has climbed out of a get-all-the-bugs-before-the-other-guy-does mentality, a 'tragedy of the commons' scenario. Those that do not observe the local rules are punished by their peers. It works, but it can get violent at times. In the summer of 2009 lobstermen sunk three of their competitors' boats at the dock in Owl's Head Harbor. Out on remote Matinicus Island, one lobsterman shot another in the neck, in part over territory. The man lived. Months later the lobsterman with the gun was acquitted with a self-defence plea.

Meanwhile, as the landings of *Homarus americanus* have steadily increased, scientists and environmentalists have consistently predicted a devastating crash. In 1973 Luis Marden in *National Geographic* worried that 'this delectable gift from the sea is in danger of disappearing, not from the bed of the ocean, perhaps, but quite possibly from our tables'.[42] Steven Murawski, a biologist at the National Marine Fisheries Service, said in 1988 that 'there's no way in God's green earth that these catches could be sustainable'.[43] The Monterey Bay Aquarium's 'Seafood Watch' guide, one created specifically for the Northeast of the United States, does not even list American lobsters as one of their 'best choices' in 2010, recommending instead spiny lobsters flown in from Florida or California. They list *Homarus*

Working in a lobster cannery in New Brunswick, Canada, 1959. Women have been a large part of the workforce in lobster canneries since the 19th century.

americanus only as a 'good alternative'.[44] Ironically, they use an illustration of the American lobster on the cover of this guide. (One concern of theirs is the threat of lobster gear to severely endangered whales.)

If anything there are actually *too many* lobsters in the waters of Maine and the Maritimes, at least in terms of the market. Canadians have invested a great deal in developing the ability to process lobsters: frozen tails and a whole range of products. These Canadian companies buy up the lobster caught by Canadian and American fishermen when they can't sell it in their local markets, then the companies store it in sprawling facilities. The Canadian companies sell their processed lobster all year round to the US, Europe and Asia. They supply casinos, cruise ships and seafood chain restaurants such as Red Lobster. They have even found a pharmaceutical and biomedical demand

A young man holding a large Caribbean spiny lobster off Mona Island, Puerto Rico, 1997.

for the vast numbers of previously discarded shells, which includes use in wound-care products and surgical drapes.

Canadian fishermen consistently catch millions more bugs than us lobstermen. The 'Maine' lobsters shipped around the world are often from Canadian fishermen, and when you order lobster tails, lobster linguini or lobster sushi at a restaurant, whether in London, Moscow, Chicago or Tokyo, you might very well be getting spiny or slipper lobster meat – which, to most palates, is by no means inferior – though to others, notably Alexandre Dumas in 1870, 'the spiny lobster is not so finely flavoured and not so highly prized'.[45]

Just as sailing vessels once opened up markets for Norwegian lobstermen and canning once opened up markets for trap fishermen in Nova Scotia, freezing technology and air shipping has probably done more to affect world lobster populations and lobster fisheries than any advancement in fishing gear or strategy of management. The ability to freeze and ship to match international demand expanded trade for fishermen in areas rich in spiny lobsters, such as Western Australia and Brazil, allowing them to compete with clawed lobster fishermen. High prices from tourists and the opportunity to sell to lucrative foreign markets encouraged small artisan spiny and slipper lobster fishermen in remote areas in the Caribbean and across the southern hemisphere to fish once pristine coastlines all too thoroughly. Some of these newer fisheries are in it for the long haul, however, hoping not to replicate historical boom and bust patterns. The spiny fishery off New Zealand (mostly *Jasus edwardsii*), for example, has a progressive individual transferrable quota system that seems to be working well in terms of both stocks and fishermen's profit.

To illustrate the global nature of the lobster as a luxury international commodity, I can tell you that I recently went to Pike's Place Market in Seattle on a Sunday morning in February. Displayed in ice in front of the men throwing salmon were four gigantic spiny lobster tails. 'We get them from all over', the fishmonger said. 'These? Just came in this morning. From the Dominican Republic. We make a killing before Valentine's Day. All the guys want to impress their dates. "Lobster", they say. "Get me some lobster!"'[46]

5 To Boil or Not to Boil

Arrange your lobster meat in the shape of a crown on a
platter. Put the tomatoes on top, and between them pour the
lobster butter you have just made. Glaze with sauce (step 4)
and serve. Since this dish is a trifle complicated, a novice
should not attempt it. It takes quite a cook to tackle it.
Alexandre Dumas, 1870[1]

Rockland, Maine, proclaims itself 'The Lobster Capital of the
World'. It is the largest town and primary port of lower Penobscot Bay, the centre of the lobster fishery in the United States.[2]
All across the bay and around its islands brightly coloured lobster buoys dot the surface in mesmerizing densities. Flying over
the area in a small plane on a summer day it's as if hundreds of
thousands of candies were strewn across the water from the
smashing of a zeppelin-sized piñata.

Every year since 1948 supply and demand come together in
mid-coast for a whirling crimson party: the Maine Lobster
Festival. Lasting five days in 2009 the festival hosted approximately 75,000 visitors and boiled some 8,850 kg (19,500 lb)
of lobster.[3] There are at least a dozen other lobster festivals of
various sizes and angles around the usa – from Redondo Beach,
California, to Panama City Beach, Florida. Both Boston and
Reno have staged competitions for the speed eating of lobster.
Sonya Thomas holds the current record after she downed in
twelve minutes 44 American lobsters – over 5 kg (11.3 lb) of
meat – at a contest in Kennebunk, Maine.[4] On the Fourth of
July in Bar Harbor, Maine, people gather to watch lobsters
with names such as 'Butters' and 'Suppa' race in lanes filled
with seawater. Bar Harbor got the idea from a similar event in
South Carolina.[5]

Poster for the 2009 Maine Lobster Festival by Bill Ronalds, celebrating the King of All Seafood.

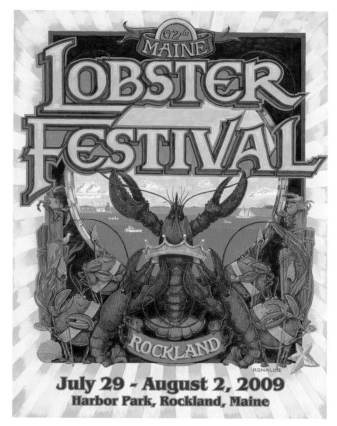

Half a dozen lobster festivals run every year in the Canadian Maritimes, too, including the 'Lobsterpalooza Feastival' in Cape Breton, Nova Scotia. The town of Shediac, New Brunswick, which refers to *itself* as the 'Lobster Capital of the World', also hosts a festival. Nova Scotia declared 2009 the 'Year of the Lobster', and their Shelburne County Lobster Festival is in the region that more humbly calls itself the 'Lobster Capital of

Enjoying lobster and the party at The Annual Dive N' Surf Redondo Beach Lobster Festival, California. With a lobster motif fork and a tool to crack the shell, this guest works to eat the clawed species (*Homarus americanus*) which has been flown in from the Canadian Maritimes or New England.

Canada'. One year the Shelburne festival featured at separate events: creamed lobsters, boiled lobsters, lobster burgers and lobster chowder. Their logo is a cartoon of a lobster in a chef's hat with a fork standing beside a terrified man in a pot of boiling water.

Yet somehow, despite these somewhat low-brow lobster hullabaloos, we, worldwide, continue to perceive the lobster as a high-end, luxury food: to be eaten on special occasions and as an experience worth travelling for. Is lobster genuinely that delicious, or are other historical, sociological and psychological factors at work?

A story is often told that early American indentured servants or slaves protested against being served lobsters too often, that they demanded various laws limiting this diet. There are indeed narratives describing lobster as so plentiful that it's not highly valued, such as the nineteenth-century account of the Canadian Maritimes by John Rowan. In 1623 William Bradford wrote that the first settlers of the Plymouth Colony could only serve newcomers 'lobster, or a peece of fish', with no bread or anything else but water.[6] Another early seventeenth-century account by William Wood declared that lobsters are 'very good fish, the small ones being the best; their plenty makes them little esteemed and seldom eaten'.[7] Yet Wood also called the lobsters 'luscious' in another section of his account. Regardless, these 'please-no-more-lobster' laws or a sense that this was *only* peasants' food – because lobster was also used for bait and fertilizer – seem greatly exaggerated, if not apocryphal. Food historian Sandy Oliver wrote that she has neither found nor heard of a single primary document of one of these complaints or ordinances against eating lobster.[8] She told me: 'I have been pounding away at this lobster question for the longest time. You'd be pretty surprised at the violence of the reactions I get. People love this myth.'[9] Oliver summarized lobster as a food in early New England: 'Like the oyster, the lobster had a dual

At Ise Ebi Matsuri, a lobster festival held at Ise-Shima in Japan, revellers parade a large spiny lobster through the streets for good fortune, and children sing and dance in the hope of a good catch. Here women fisher-divers led by a priest pray for the safety of divers. They will carry the lobster effigy into the ocean to pray to the god of the Sea.

identity as a luxury food in cities and inland where it was not native, and as a food for all classes, including poor fishermen, along the coast.'[10] In 1887, at the height of the canning era, Richard Rathbun wrote in his government report:

> On the sea coasts where [lobsters] occur, except in the vicinity of large towns and cities, they are not generally much, if any, more expensive than the common fish of the same region, and they are, therefore, quite extensively eaten by all classes, and many of the fishermen and others also catch them for their own use. Away from the sea-shore, and even in many of the larger markets located near good fishing-grounds, the prices are generally much higher, placing this class of food beyond the reach of the poorer people, and often raising it to the rank of a luxury.[11]

Of course, just as the pizza chef has difficulty eating his own pie, not all fishermen salivate at the thought of a lobster dinner. Thomas Fairfax, a nineteenth-century lobster smack captain, said: 'Lobsters are very good as an article of commerce, and pretty enough to look at, after they're b'iled; but, as to eating

Canned lobster label, Portland [Maine] Packing Company, c. 1867. Under 'Bay Lobster' the label says: 'This favorite Crustacea has become so important an article of food, that a statement of the best methods of preparing it for the table will be useful. Many prefer it cold, just as taken from the Can, it having been boiled before sealing'. The label goes on to give directions for preparing 'Lobster Curry', 'Balls', 'Salad', and 'A La Creme'.

them, I prefer castoff rubber shoes.'[12] More recently, a man named George Hoag from inland Maine said: 'If them tourists want to come up from Boston and pay them prices, then, by Christ, let 'em. Damn fools. Lobsters, hell, they're big cockroaches, that's what they are. You ain't gonna catch me eatin' one, even if I could afford the damn thing.'[13]

Yet for every Captain Fairfax and George Hoag there are thousands of people who drool over the prospect of lobster as food, who adore a quiet evening at the edge of a dock eating fresh lobsters with family and friends, or have a blast at a bustling, buttery lobster festival. Accounts abound of people positively adoring the firm, salty-but-not-*too*-fishy flesh of lobsters, along with the process of eating them out of the shell. Robert Blakey, a nineteenth-century British professor, hyperbolized:

> Only think of Adam and his immediate descendants regaling themselves on boiled lobsters, or indulging in the stimulating properties of its various forms of sauces! Who knows the part lobsters may have taken in the roystering and Bacchanalian revelries among the citizens of the Plain – how many convivial spirits were wont to gather in the evenings around its savoury fumes preparatory for whetting the appetite for more varied and sensual indulgences, ere their gluttony and other sins consigned them to Divine chastisement? Speculations crowd on the mind, in all shapes and forms, when we think of the lobster feasts before the Flood.[14]

The Greeks and Romans seemed to have enjoyed eating lobster. The Roman chef and author, Apicius, was reportedly so fond of slipper lobsters that once he heard about their size and excellence on the coast of Tunisia he mounted an expedition to sample them for himself.[15] Apicius wrote of recipes for boiled and roasted lobster, including one with a sauce made from 'pepper, cumin, rue, honey, vinegar, fish stock, and olive oil'.[16]

Though it seems shellfish fell out of favour for a good part of the Middle Ages, food historian Terence Scully explained that European nobles and affluent townspeople ate and could afford lobster.[17] The Vatican's fifteenth-century recipe book of the master cook to King Charles V includes a few mentions of lobster, such as directions for preparing *Gravé de d'escrevisses*, which seems to have been for either the clawed or spiny species. This *gravé* is a thick, spiced sauce made of lobster, which is then poured over fried chunks of lobster meat.[18] Another mediaeval recipe book recommended that when preparing rissoles one could substitute lobster for meat on days when the Church required it to be a 'lean-day'.[19]

Lobster was a small but present feature of the diet in England's Early Modern period.[20] Robert May included over a dozen lobster recipes in his 1678 edition of *The Accomplisht Cook*. He wrote directions for stewing lobster in wine, mincing with eels, marinating, roasting on a spit, broiling and jellying lobsters, as well as how to 'boil Lobsters to eat cold the common way' and how to 'keep Lobsters a quarter of a year very good', by wrapping the cooked corpses in brine-soaked rags and burying them in sand down in the cellar.[21] The poet Alexander Pope used lobster to evoke decadent times in his poem 'A Farewell to London in the Year 1715'. He wrote of he and his colleagues' rakish excesses in the city: 'Luxurious lobster-nights, farewell,/For sober, studious days.'[22]

Hannah Glasse's popular *The Art of Cookery Made Plain and Easy* (first London edition 1747), had half a dozen recipes for lobsters and lobster roe, including lobster in fish sauce and lobster pie. Glasse recommended that when at the market: 'Chuse them by their weight; the heaviest are best, if no water be in them [;] if new, the tail will pull smart, like a spring.'[23] *The Compleat Housewife* (*c.* 1729) also gives a few lobster recipes, including one for pickling, one for 'potting' a dozen boiled lobsters in butter and spices so the meat will keep for a month or more and a recipe for roasting: 'Tie your lobsters to the spit alive, baste them with water and salt till they look very red.'[24] This also from *The Compleat Housewife*:

> To butter Crabs or Lobsters.
> YOUR crabs and lobsters being boiled and cold, take all the meat out of the shells and body, break the claws, and take out all their meat, mince it small, and put it altogether, adding to it two or three spoonfuls of claret, a very little vinegar, a nutmeg grated; let it boil up till it is thorough hot; then put in some butter melted, with some anchovies and gravy, and thicken with the yolks of an egg or two; when it is very hot put it in the large shell, and stick it with toasts.[25]

In the nineteenth century, with the introduction of canning and improved transportation methods, lobster became a more accessible dish. Live lobsters were still cooked and served, but recipes now regularly involved picked lobster meat and often recommended it served cold in lobster salads.

Charles Dickens wrote often about Victorian food, including lobster. In *David Copperfield* (1850), for example, the honourable Peggotty family on the coast 'dealt in lobsters, crabs, and craw-fish', and they bring David two 'prodigious' lobsters, among other shellfish, as a gift when visiting him at school. Later David is jealous of a suitor offering a picnic meal of lobster to his beloved Dora, and when Traddles tells of living well in London he speaks of simply picking up a lobster on the way home from

According to food historian Sandy Oliver, this was the most common way to serve lobster in the Victorian Era: a 'genteel form, neatly trimmed and garnished'.

the theatre.[26] In an edition of Dickens's periodical *Household Words* an article explains how to make a proper lobster salad for a supper-party. Lobster salad is presented as a normal dish, almost obligatory for a ball supper that is 'good, economical, and easily prepared'. The author suggests fresh-picked meat mixed with hard-boiled egg yolks to be piled high atop 'perfectly dry' lettuce, with a creamy dressing or mayonnaise sauce.[27] In another issue of *Household Words*, a writer gives this recipe, intended in part for the middle-class reader:

POTATO CASE WITH LOBSTER
Steam and mash up a pound of potatoes very smooth and dry. Add to this the yolks of two eggs, work over the fire in a stew-pan until dry, then mould in the same manner as a pork-pie crust, brush it over with yolk of egg, and bake until nicely coloured. With a quarter of a pint of

white sauce mix half a teaspoonful of essence of anchovy and one of lemon juice, stir into it half a tin of preserved lobster, and let it stand by the side of the fire to get hot, but do not let it boil. Fresh lobster can be used, of course, but is more expensive. When ready, pour the lobster with its sauce, which should be thick, into the case and serve.[28]

Dickens's wife, Catherine, also wrote of lobsters in her *What Shall We Have for Dinner?* (1851). She advocated lobster prepared in several different ways, even for the same party. She suggested lobster cutlets, fillets, lobster salad, lobster curry and diced claw meat to add to a seafood filling for puff-pastry.[29]

Dozens of recipes and menus with lobster in all sorts of forms appeared in other Victorian cookbooks and in restaurants on both sides of the Atlantic. Authors such as Eliza Acton and Mrs D. A. Lincoln, in various editions, explained preparations for lobster patties, salads, sausages, lobsters in soups, chowders, bisques and lobsters sautéed in butter with a little flour, chili-vinegar and nutmeg, then served in the shell. They recommended the use of the eggs, the 'coral', for a variety of sauces, and wrote

A 'Shell-fish', awaiting the dressing room, in Eliza Acton's *Modern Cookery for Private Families* (1868).

Dressed Lobster.

'Dressed Lobster' in Acton's *Modern Cookery* (1868). Acton explains: 'Before a lobster is sent to table take off the large claws, hold each of them firmly with the edge upwards, and with a quick light blow from a cutlet bat or ought else convenient for the purpose, crack the shell without disfiguring the fish. Split the tail open with a very sharp knife and dish the lobster in the manner shown in the engraving, either with, or without a napkin under it'.

about how to make devilled lobster, 'Indian lobster-cutlets' and lobster fricasseed.[30] A menu for Keeler's European Hotel in inland Albany, New York, for example, had in March of 1897 an image of a lobster at the top of the menu, even though they offered twice as many oyster dishes. The entrees included lobsters 'Plain Boiled' and 'Extra Plain Boiled', lobsters broiled alive, lobster croquettes with peas, and 'Patties a la Keeler'.[31]

As overfishing and over-canning began depleting the stocks of lobster, the price went up accordingly. It became difficult for a family to buy lobster if living away from the coast, and thus its status rose as a luxury food. An author in 1905 wrote: 'With lobsters at 30 cents a pound they are quite beyond my reach; and all I can do is dream of the time when they sold for 5, and we had all the lobsters we could eat.'[32]

Since then lobster has remained a food symbolic of the prosperous and served primarily on special occasions. This is reflected nicely in the 2005 film *Brooklyn Lobster* in which a New York family struggles to keep its lobster pound and sea-food market from being bought out. Here lobsters are a direct metaphor for money. The film opens with the pound's loss of saltwater circulation, so all of the lobsters, ready for the Christmas rush, are in danger of dying. Keeping the lobsters alive throughout the film parallels the family's struggle to save the business. The owner, Frank Giorgio (Danny Aiello), identifies personally with the pugnacity of these animals but, more importantly, lobsters are his livelihood. One of his employees calls the boxes of lobsters 'crates of cash'. The wealthy WASP characters in the movie eat lobsters loudly, almost grotesquely, while wearing plastic bibs over formal clothes – ties, blue blazers, pearls – and speak rowdily about it as a special food. One rich, duplicitous character shouts multiple times: 'Bring me a big f—ing lobster!' The film shows several close-ups of lobsters, but the first one of a cooked bug, a bright red full-screen image of a lobster boiling in a pot, is held just after the family gets the news that their business has been saved. The Giorgio

One of Freeman McKown's popular clambakes in West Boothbay Harbor, Maine, in which lobster was always the centrepiece. McKown ran these events from about 1890 to 1930.

In the 2005 film *Brooklyn Lobster*, Christmastime is a crucial money-making season for this lobster supplier – so they fly a 'Santa Claws' to advertise.

family rarely eats lobsters but in the end, when they do, it is at their Christmas and celebration dinner. Notably, this blue-collar family, their employees and their friends do not wear bibs at their civilized, joyous feast.[33]

Sexual connotations have regularly been stirred in with the lobster's status as expensive, decadent fare. Each year the Maine Lobster Festival crowns a pretty young local woman as the Maine Sea Goddess. She sits centre stage in a throne with a large green claw over each shoulder. Allegedly Alexander the Great so craved lobsters that the members of his court needed this food, either whole or as a sauce, to 'allay his periodical paroxysms of passion'.[34] In 1620 Dr Tobias Venner, in his *Via Recta ad Vitam Longam*, believed lobster to be an aphrodisiac. He advised that it 'giveth much good and firme nourishment' but one should be careful because lobster 'maketh a great propensitie unto venereall embracements'.[35] Venner's views might have just been due to the food's expense and rarity – as might be true today. [36]

This association of lobster with lust and sexual activity seems to have carried on through the centuries. John Smith wrote in 'A Rhapsody upon a Lobster' (1713):

The Lusty Food helps Female Neighbours,
Promotes their Husband's, and their Labours;
And in return much Work supplies
For that Bright Midwife of the Skies.
Lobster with *Cavear* in fit Places,
Gives won'drous Help in barren Cases;
It warms the chiller Veins, and proves
A kind Incentive to our Loves;
It is a Philter, and High Diet,
That lets no Lady sleep in Quiet.[37]

A few years later poet John Gay composed 'To a Young Lady', in which the narrator sends a gift of an aphrodisiac (a lamprey) to a maid he is courting. An aunt explains to the young woman that the man is trying to seduce her. In explaining these types of foods, she says: 'If I eat lobster, 'tis so warming,/That every man I see looks charming'. The narrator ends:

In this, I own, your aunt is clear;
I sent you what I well might spare:
For when I see you, (without joking,)
Your eyes, lips, breasts, are so provoking;
They set my heart more cock-a-hoop,
Than could whole seas of cray-fish soup.[38]

Chef Jasper White explained the lobster's allure this way: 'It is the briny-sweet taste of the sea, where all life began, that is so intensely satisfying and sensually stimulating.'[39] Beyond the often feminine ascriptions to the ocean and *her* creatures, there is also perhaps something sexual going on visually, sub-consciously, with the bright red at the table, as a food, as a quencher of carnal appetite: think red heart, Valentine's Day, red silk sheets, women in red dresses, lips, nipples and so forth. Lord Byron, though surely no exemplar, wrote in a letter that 'a woman should never be seen eating or drinking, unless it be *lobster sallad & Champagne*, the only truly feminine & becoming viands'.[40]

In the early decades of the twentieth century New York restaurant owners created luxurious establishments with elaborate interiors called 'lobster palaces'. Around Times Square and Broadway these palaces served champagne and lobster late at night, after the theatre. Lobster was especially expensive, and here wealthy society could mingle with showgirls and the theatre crowd, the rich and the famous. The palaces were sensual, high-publicity restaurants that winked at covert trysts and men's parties in private rooms. Historian Lewis Erenberg wrote: 'The lobster palaces, as they were called because of their gilded interiors and gay late-night lobster suppers, merchandised an opulent experience of material pleasure and hoped-for naughtiness.'[41] Around this time an older wealthy man with a young attractive woman on his arm, whom we might call a 'sugar daddy' today, was known as 'a lobster'.[42]

A lobster dinner paired with sex is common in contemporary popular culture, too. As film-critic and oceanographer Andrew Fisher has pointed out, the scene in *Flashdance* (1983), where the young dancer (Jennifer Beals) salaciously sucks on lobster meat while she moves her foot under the table to stroke the crotch of her date, perhaps inspired a similar scene in the romantic comedy *Splash*, released the following year.[43] In *Splash* the sexually uninhibited mermaid (Daryl Hannah) lustily eats her lobster right through the shell, crunching as Allen (Tom Hanks) tries to propose marriage to her at a fancy restaurant. As the formal guests in suits and sparkling gowns steal glances, she says: 'That's how we eat lobster where I come from.'[44]

Overleaf:
The lascivious allure of the lobster is shown in Pierre Outin's 1870s *Stealing a Kiss.*

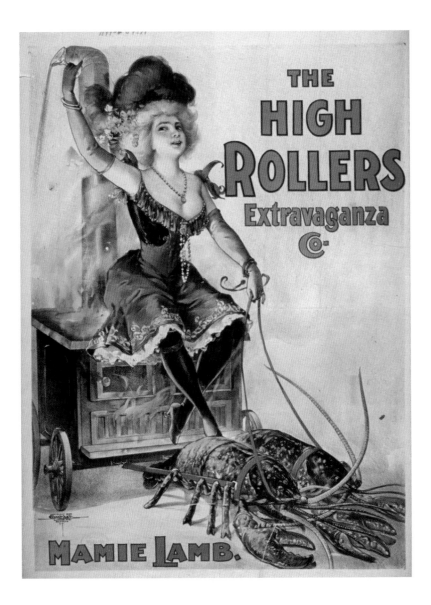

Daryl Hannah in *Splash* (dir. Ron Howard, 1984) is a sexy mermaid who, unaware of cultural norms 'on land', crunches straight into the shell of a lobster at a fancy dinner.

Previous page: An 1890s American theatre poster that evokes sex, money and absurdity, presumably for some type of burlesque show. The erotic, sadistic pun here is that a 'lobster' at this time was a name for an older, wealthy man – a high roller – who wined and dined showgirls, often with a lobster dinner.

An ideal example is in a pulp novel by Shirley Jump titled *The Angel Craved Lobster* (2005) in which a young woman named Meredith moves to Boston from a small farming town in Indiana. She wants to lose her virginity with a variety of new experiences, but she falls in love instead. By the end of the novel, the man, who won't indulge her lust because she is too special, proposes marriage to her over the lobster dinner that he'd been promising for most of the story. The novel includes seafood recipes throughout, narrated by different characters. As we reach the climax of the book (loss of virginity and engagement), Jump writes, slathered with double entendre:

Meredith's When-the-Mood-Is-Right Lobster Stew

3 tablespoons butter
1 pound lobster meat
1 cup heavy cream
3 cups milk
1/2 teaspoon salt
1/4 teaspoon white pepper
Paprika

An illustration by Dahlov Ipcar for her 1962 children's book, *Lobsterman*. This lobstering family has no anxiety about boiling the animals alive.

Pull out all the stops now with the most decadent dish you can create. This one is rich . . . in everything you've been denying yourself. Melt the butter and fry the lobster meat until it's warm and heated through. Add the cream and milk, gradually, stirring it carefully over low to medium-low heat. Don't rush it! The end result will be worth every second you put into it. Season with salt and pepper, then let this simmer gently for about 15 to 20 minutes. Sprinkle a little paprika on top. Since this dish is so indulgent, be careful who you serve it to. He might just come back for seconds. And thirds. And . . . *more*.[45]

Lobster as a food is unique due to a combination of factors. It remains a meal for the wealthy or something special for someone of average means. Away from the ocean lobster might be considered as indulgent as caviar or filet mignon. Clawed lobster has been a regular dish at the White House[46] – a reminder that it is one of the few dishes that North America can claim as superior to other parts of the world, and geographically privileged for its larger specimens. A few lobster recipes cooked at five-star restaurants are so famous that you probably recognize them by name, such as Lobster Newburg, Lobster Thermidor and Lobster Fra Diavolo. Even today in Rockland, Maine, in August, a take-out lobster roll costs four times more than a large fully stacked cheeseburger in a fast food restaurant (a fact infuriating and befuddling to most lobstermen getting very little from the wholesaler). The shell of a cooked lobster is colourful and adds serious pizzazz to any table. Lobster is caught wild and does better than nearly all other fisheries from most environmentalists' perspectives. It is a nutritious food, at least excluding the melted butter. The approximately 100 gm (3.5 oz) of meat you get from a 450 gm (1 lb) lobster has fewer than 100 calories, and it has less cholesterol and fat than the same amount of skinless chicken or turkey breast. Lobster meat also comes with a nice portion of omega-3 acids, which are commended these days as good for our hearts.[47] Lobster has been called 'the *ultimate* white meat'.

When you're presented with a whole bug, however, this food is cumbersome and messy. Lobster 'in the rough' is an event. Lobster is also one of the few animals in most modern homes that is purchased alive – with two eyes and with two claws unavoidably likened to human hands. The live lobster in the kitchen or cooked on the plate is a final vestige of what it is like to butcher or kill our own food. Other than crabs, Louisiana crawfish and a few small fish species, nearly all other animal foods are cooked and cleaned, headless and limbless, before most diners in developed countries ever see them in the market or on their plate. Lobster as a food is therefore fraught with contemporary ethical dilemmas.

The belief that boiling a lobster alive for best taste and safety goes back to the ancient Romans. In the fifteenth century, Platina wrote: 'This animal alone does not have good flesh unless it is cooked alive in boiling water.'[48] This has carried into modern times, as exemplified by French author and chef Dr Edouard de Pomiane who remembered in the 1930s how plentiful and cheap the clawed (*homard*) and spiny (*langouste*) lobsters once were off the coast of Brittany. He ate them every day and prepared them differently each time. He believed that boiling the lobster alive was best – 'one must admit that no complicated method of preparation is half as good as fresh-caught lobster simply boiled in sea water, cooled and served with mayonnaise' – yet he took the time in his instructions to tell you to 'plunge the live lobster into fast-boiling water so that its sufferings shall be as brief as possible'.[49] A dish like 'Homard à l'Américaine', which he thought too rich because it drowns out the taste of the lobster, requires the animal to be cut into pieces while still alive. Pomiane directed you to plunge a sharp knife in the lobster's head, which he believed kills it instantly.

Fig. 24. Lobster Américaine *(1)*.
Cut the live lobster into even-sized pieces following the joints. Hold firmly in the left hand.

Fig. 28.
To split a cooked rock or spiny lobster, cut the tail open first, then the head and the body. Use a knife with a strong blade.

Photographic instructions in a French cookbook showing how to prepare lobsters, both *homard* (clawed) and *langouste* (spiny); aspiring cooks are told that 'the lobster must be alive' before cutting it into pieces.

Woody Allen in *Annie Hall* (dir. Allen, 1977) shows how the inability to face cooking a lobster alive can stand for a lack of masculinity.

Yet the boiling of the lobster alive has been a preoccupation of modern eaters, as evidenced by the joke gifts sold in Rockland or some of the floats and costumes at the festival's parade. Author David Foster Wallace gave a characteristically cerebral and cynical account of the Maine Lobster Festival in a 2004 issue of *Gourmet*. He comments on how a western beef festival would never include any giant slaughterhouse floor or anything the equivalent of the 'World's Largest Lobster Cooker', where you can watch your dinner steamed alive – perhaps, as Wallace put it, like some sort of 'Roman circus or medieval torture-fest'.[50]

Films such as *Annie Hall* (1977) and *Julie & Julia* (2009) both feature scenes of frantic, comic attempts to get over the fear of putting living lobsters into a pot at home. These two movies include the killing of lobster as related to gender roles. In *Annie Hall* the first scene of a young couple having fun together is at a beach house, trying to put the lobsters in the pot after they have escaped the bag and are crawling over the kitchen floor. Annie (Diane Keaton) is the first one who eventually handles the lobster, but Alvy (Woody Allen) actually drops it in the boiling water. Later in the film the scene is replicated with another girlfriend but here the woman mocks Alvy for not being able to boil it without a fuss: 'They're only lobsters. Look, you're a grown man, you know how to pick up a lobster.'[51] The scene in *Julie & Julia*, based on a chapter titled 'They Shoot Lobsters, Don't They?' in Julie Powell's memoir of the same name, has Julie's husband (Chris Messina) come into the kitchen to rescue her while she whimpers, frightened, in the living room. The lobsters in their death throes had literally flung off the lid. The husband slams the lid back on, holding it there proudly. In contrast, during another scene in the film, Julia Child (Meryl Streep) first proves herself in France by unabashedly cleaving a live *homard* while the male culinary students cower behind her. One telling difference between these two films is actually in the credits, because the latter ends with a mention of the American Humane Association. In turns out that although many lobsters were sacrificed to make the lobster dishes for other scenes in the movie, AHA members monitored the filming of the boiling alive scene in *Julie & Julia*. The lobsters weren't actually dropped into a killer pot. It was a cool mist that supplied the 'steam'.[52]

The concern with the morality of boiling a lobster alive goes back to at least the nineteenth century in Western culture, as exemplified by Baron Bolland's parodic poem 'The Negro's Dying Blush' (1835) and the writings of the humanitarians at the turn of the twentieth century who debated as to whether or not the lobster feels a level of pain that we as supposedly sensitive, caring people should avoid.[53] The dilemma can become a question more for philosophers than scientists, although several experts claim a kinder method of killing a lobster. Dozens of scientific experiments have been conducted since about 1915, if not earlier.[54] The studies almost all involve killing a bunch of lobsters in different ways – often comparing boiling to variations of chopping, freezing, saltwater immersion and/or slow boiling from cold water – and then monitoring the doomed

Cover of PETA flyer as part of a 1999 'Let lobsters live!' campaign. On the other side actress Mary Tyler Moore is quoted: 'A lobster who is being boiled alive will frantically scrape the sides of the pot trying to escape the pain … To me, eating a lobster is out of the question.'

lobsters' responses in ever more complex methods. After killing some 54 lobsters in four different ways, marine biologist Elizabeth Murray of Oxford concluded in 1962: 'From the point of view of kindness to the lobster, it is hard to say which is the best method of killing, because it is impossible, and probably will always be impossible, to say whether the lobster is suffering pain or not. Therefore, to give the animal the benefit of the doubt, the quickest methods are probably the best.'[55] Is the real question, to be honest with ourselves, not *how* it is done, but more, *if* we should kill the animal at all? Which plunges us briskly into much larger questions of ranking animals, vegetarianism and animal rights.

In Wallace's article, titled 'Consider the Lobster', he goes back and forth about the issue. He considers how cruelly other animals are treated for our food, the neuroscience involved with pain and the lobster's nervous system, the very definition of pain, the inconvenience of even having to consider that what he's doing is ethically wrong and trying to resolve for himself the ever-contradictory remarks by all sides. Each year representatives from the People for the Ethical Treatment of Animals (PETA) protest at the Maine Lobster Festival. He wrote that he heard a woman once got half-naked and painted herself like a lobster to call attention to the injustice. Wallace arrived here:

> Suffice to say that both the scientific and the philosophical arguments on either side of the animal-suffering issue are involved, abstruse, technical, often informed by self-interest or ideology, and in the end so totally inconclusive that as a practical matter, in the kitchen or the restaurant, it all still seems to come down to individual conscience, going with (no pun) your gut.[56]

During one of the annual Maine Lobster Festival parades in Rockland, Maine, representatives for PETA protest against what they believe to be the inhumane killing of lobsters.

6 Lobster Tales

Among the rock ledges, eels and cunners forage greedily,
while the lobster feels his way with nimble wariness through
the perpetual twilight.
Rachel Carson, 1937[1]

Once there was a Hawaiian boy named Pu-nia who lived on the
Big Island alone with his mother. His father had been eaten by Kai-
ale-ale, the King of the Sharks, while diving for lobsters. Kai-ale-
ale and ten other sharks voraciously guarded a special cave where
the prized animals lived. Since his father's death, the boy often
heard his mother pine for some lobster to go with their potatoes.
So one morning Pu-nia decided *he* would catch lobster for her.

Pu-nia stood at the edge of the sea. Pretending he did not
know the sharks were awake and could hear him, he said: 'Here
am I, Pu-nia, and I am going into the cave to get lobsters for
myself and my mother. That great shark, Kai-ale-ale, is asleep
now, and I can dive to the point over there, and then go into
the cave; I will take two lobsters in my hands, and my mother
and I will have something to eat with our sweet potatoes.'[2]
Pu-nia took a rock and threw it toward the point where he said
he was planning to dive. All of the sharks frenzied around the
splash, foaming and bubbling the sea, while Pu-nia dived in from
another point, swimming down past the corals and the colours
of the reef and down into the dark cave. With his bare hands the
boy collected two heavy lobsters in the dim light. He knew how
to seize the animals and hold them so the spines didn't make
him bleed. Then he swam back to the surface and climbed onto
the shore before the sharks realized they'd been tricked.

In Juliette May
Fraser's 1924
illustration to
a traditional
Hawaiian story,
the lobster is the
prize for a heroic,
death-defying
young fisherman.

128

"*Then Pu-nia dived . . . into the cave, took two lob-sters in his hands, and came up on the place that he had spoken from.*"

Now in the sun, Pu-nia admired his two lobsters – their glistening white stripes and spots and the bright orange at the base of their antennae. Pu-nia spoke directly to Kai-ale-ale. 'It was the one with the thin tail, that showed Pu-nia what to do.' While the boy brought the prize back to his mother, the King of the Sharks found the traitor with the thinnest tail and had him killed and eaten.

Pu-nia and his mother feasted. When they were hungry again, the boy returned and played the same trick. He tossed a rock in a different direction, swam down to the cave, grabbed two lobsters and was back ashore before the sharks realized what happened. This time the boy told Kai-ale-ale: 'It was the one with the big stomach that told Pu-nia what to do.' Kai-ale-ale killed and ate the shark with the largest stomach.

The boy continued to fool them, gathering lobsters when-ever he and his mother were hungry. Eventually all of the sharks had been killed and only Kai-ale-ale remained.

The boy knew that the rock trick wouldn't work with the King of the Sharks alone, so he collected two poles of hardwood from the forest, and he filled a bag with sticks and charcoal. At the edge of the shore, the boy told Kai-ale-ale that if he chewed Pu-nia up, if his blood rose to the surface, his mother would be able to bring him back to life. The boy then gripped his wood and bag, took a great breath, and sliced into the sea toward the lobster cave. Kai-ale-ale, thinking himself the smarter, swallowed the boy whole so there would be no blood.

Now inside the belly of the shark, Pu-nia managed to prop up its mouth with the poles. He built a fire inside the shark's stomach. Kai-ale-ale swam frantically through the ocean. When they got closer to land, the boy told the shark that if he swam to the breaking surf, Pu-nia would be saved, but if the shark took him to a sandy beach, Pu-nia would die. The great shark, fooled once again, rushed madly to the sandy cove in a final attempt to kill Pu-nia. The shark beached itself. The boy rushed out of its mouth and shouted, 'Kai-ale-ale, Kai-ale-ale, the King of the Sharks, has come to visit us!' The islanders arrived with spears and knives and summarily killed their nemesis. So ends the traditional Hawaiian story 'The Boy Pu-nia and the King of the Sharks'.

Author and ethnographer Padraic Colum finishes his version of 'Pu-nia' this way:

> Every day after that, Pu-nia was able to go down into the cave and get lobsters for himself and his mother. And all the people rejoiced when they knew that the eleven sharks that guarded the cave had been got rid of by the boy Pu-nia.[3]

The 'Pu-nia' story is a perfect example of lobsters in literature and the arts: our crustacean heroes in a vital, albeit supporting role. Alas, we lobsterologists in our littoral lobster libraries have no opus. Lobsterdom may boast no *Moby-Crawfish* or 'Rime of the Ancient Lobsterman'. Benchley and Spielberg gave us no blockbuster movie *Claws*, and Blake offered us no verse 'Lobstyr, Lobstyr, boiling bright'. There is yet no lobster Bambi, Flipper or Pooh Bear.

The 'Pu-nia' story, derived from the oral tradition, connects a series of surprisingly disparate works of literature written in English, and it highlights the three primary approaches, settings of a sort, to which writers and artists have taken us when describing these animals: depicting the lobster underneath the water, showing the lobster breaking the surface as the prize for a heroic fisherman, and using the lobster on land to serve as a variety of symbols. It's a literary taxonomy that has some slosh

A 1480s woodcut printed in a German translation of a book of Indian animal fables by Bidpai. This fable is a rare instance in which a smart crustacean gets the better of a situation. Notice the claw around the bird's neck.

Jesse Wilcox Smith's 'Tom reached down the hole after him' illustrates a scene in Charles Kingsley's 1863 *The Water-Babies* in which the water-baby crawls into an inkwell-style pot in an attempt to save an old lobster.

over the edges, but that's no different from the lobster's biological organization. It's how I organize my lobster library, anyhow.

A recent version as a children's book by Lee Wardlaw, *Punia and the King of the Sharks* (1997), features lobsters prominently. In the opening paragraph the sharks say: 'We must keep these lobsters for ourselves', and the narrator describes the lobsters as 'fat' and 'sweet as coconut'.[4] Wardlaw's illustrator, Felipe Dávalos, paints the lobsters within a bright coral reef ecosystem, using their striped antennae in nearly every image. Dávalos's lobsters have large, sensitive eyes, rendering them cute and inquisitive.

Only a few other authors and artists have worked with the lobster beneath the surface in any imaginative fashion. You may borrow from my lobster library, for example, a comical nineteenth-century yarn about 'sagacious' lobsters crawling a hundred miles, finding their way home after escaping from a wrecked lobster smack.[5] An old Portuguese legend tells of a lobster retrieving a dropped holy cross for a Catholic priest, actually delivering it to him on an island after a storm: 'The Father, falling on his knees, took his crucifix, after which the lobster-fish returned to the sea.'[6]

Charles Kingsley wrote a children's fantasy novel, *The Water-Babies* (1863), in which he describes a 'distinguished' lobster living off the coast of England. When Tom, the water-baby (possessing powers similar to Pu-nia), first sees the lobster he thinks it 'odd'. The narrator says:

> All the ingenious men, and all the scientific men, and all the fanciful men, in the world, with all the old German bogy-painters into the bargain, could never invent, if all their wits were boiled into one, anything so curious, and so ridiculous, as a lobster.[7]

Though the lobster and Tom can speak, Kingsley tried to be accurate with his ecological descriptions, teaching his young readers. He describes the lobster's quick backward movements into gaps between the rocks, the lobster's separate 'knobbed' and 'jagged' claw, and the feeding methods of the gooseneck barnacles living on its shell. Later, Tom finds the lobster caught in a pot. He gets pulled into the trap trying to help, but a blood-thirsty otter swims in, too. The lobster protects Tom with his claws, eventually killing the otter, allowing Tom to escape. But then, just as Tom again tries to free the lobster, a fisherman pulls up the pot. The lobster manages to free himself at the boat's rail by giving a 'tremendous snap', relinquishing his claw, and falling back into the sea.[8] By helping another creature, Tom is now allowed to find other water-babies. His charity to the lobster pays off: a subtle lesson here to be kind to lobsters.

A few poets have worked with the lobster underwater, notably Anne Sexton and George Mackay Brown, who both wrote poems titled 'Lobster' as part of bestiary collections. Sexton's poem, first published in 1973, features a solitary lobster, probably *Homarus americanus* since Sexton was from the Boston area and the animal in her poem is captured while the 'U.S.A. sleeps'. Sexton's lobster is under the surface and alive, 'A shoe with legs,/a stone dropped from heaven', who crawls on the bottom, doing 'mournful' work. The lobster is ignorant of the simple events, tragedies and crimes that occupy mankind ashore. Sexton pities her lobster, describing him as old a second time, to complete her poem this way:

He is the old hunting dog of the sea
who in the morning will rise from it
and be undrowned
and they will take his perfect green body
and paint it red.[9]

George Mackay Brown wrote his 'Lobster' a decade later, focusing on the metaphor of the lobster's shell as his armour. Brown grew up around creel fishermen on the Orkney Islands, so the lobster in his mind's eye is *Homarus gammarus*.[10] His lobster is solitary, proud and long-lived. Here age is a point of honour, befitting the time of its species on earth and the perception of ancient and more spiritually centred cultures of the East. Brown was in his mid-sixties when he wrote the poem. Here it is in full:

LOBSTER

What are you doing here
Samurai
In the west, in the sunset streams of the west?

How you lord it over those peasants,
The whelks
The mussels and the shrimps and scallops.

There you clank, in dark blue armour
Along the ocean floor,
With the shadows flowing over you,
Haddock, mackerel,
And the sun the shadow of a big yellow whale.

Nothing stands in your way, swashbuckler.

The orchards where you wander
Drop sufficient plunder,
Mercenary in the dark blue coat of mail.

Be content, be content far out
With the tides' bounty,
Going from smithy to smithy, in your season
For an ampler riveting.

Fold your big thumbs,
Under the trembling silver-blue scales of the moon.[11]

For my money Brown's poem is the most beautiful piece of writing about the lobster in English, and if there's hope for a classic work of lobster literature I humbly put this one forward. The poem smoothly and simply mixes anthropomorphism – the lobster as lord, warrior and pirate – with ecological accuracy: how the lobster moults, its habitat, other creatures and its claws. I adore Brown's use of sun and moonlight underwater and the primary onomatopoeic word in the poem: *clank*. Historical war helmets and armour, such as those constructed with overlapping plates to cover the neck, were once called 'lobster-tailed'.[12] Brown evokes in 'Lobster' the immortal sea, in tune with the moon's cycles and, after layering imagery of ancient battles, he leaves the reader with the lobster in a peaceful, meditative posture. Brown, like Sexton, seems to envy the lobster's indifference (like the sea) to the troubles of people, and he wishes to keep the animal safe. For Sexton, the cause is lost; for Brown, hope remains. Brown speaks in the second-person to the lobster, advising it to stay away from the trap, as if to tell the animal: be satisfied with what you have, my venerable friend.

Albrecht Dürer, *Lobster*, 1495, ink drawing. Dürer's accurate illustration of a European lobster gives the animal a fierce, dignified appearance, almost like a Greco-Roman warrior, due in part to its prominent rostrum, active legs and the claws open and anticipatory.

In 'Pu-nia' the young hero becomes a legendary fisherman
of lobsters through cleverness and by working alone in the face
of paralysing danger. In the eyes of several writers and artists
the lobsterman has similar traits to this Polynesian boy: he or
she often works alone, expertly, fearless of the ocean's hazards.
The lobsterman is regularly depicted as a different breed, a little
better than the rest of us.

One of the earlier literary celebrations of the lobsterman is
by Walt Whitman, who while extolling all manner of maritime
trades with his usual exuberance writes in 'A Song of Joys' from
Leaves of Grass (1881):

> I pull the wicker pots up slantingly, the dark green lob-
>   sters are desperate with their claws as I take them out,
>   I insert wooden pegs in the joints of their pincers,
> I go to all the places one after another, and then row back
>   to the shore,

There in a huge kettle of boiling water the lobsters shall
be boil'd till their color becomes scarlet.[13]

Whitman was born on Long Island and spent many of his early
years there, not far from John Whittaker's fishing grounds.

In the century that follows Whitman's *Leaves of Grass*, a
series of narratives about coastal life explain period details of
lobster fishing and reveal our society's changing perception of
the lobsterman. The majority of these were written by women,
and include five must-haves for your bug bookshelf: Sarah Orne
Jewett's *The Country of the Pointed Firs* (1896), Leo Walmsley's
Three Fevers (1932) and *Phantom Lobster* (1933), Louise Dickinson Rich's *The Peninsula* (1958) and Linda Greenlaw's *The
Lobster Chronicles* (2002).

In her short stories Jewett describes lobster as a food and even
briefly includes a lobster cannery, but in her most famous work,
her autobiographical novella *Pointed Firs*, lobstering, lobster
pots and lobster smacks are subtle strands of a small maritime

Author Leo
Walmsley
photographed
a father and
his two sons
lobstering off
Robin Hood's
Bay, Yorkshire,
c. 1932. The fish-
ermen here are
likely the main
characters in
Walmsley's books.

community beside the mouth of Penobscot Bay. Jewett depicts a town at the end of the nineteenth century after the Lobster Rush has blown through, a community in decline, with lobstering a part-time fishery. At the end of *Pointed Firs*, as the narrator leaves the town on a ferry after her summer of visiting and writing, her final image of the coast includes an almost anachronistic, widowed old fisherman tending his pots. Although perhaps laced with pity, Jewett's lobsterman is an independent figure, living dangerously, deserving of respect.

Across the Atlantic on the Yorkshire coast, author Leo Walmsley wrote about the revitalization of the lobster industry in his 1930s autobiographical novel *Three Fevers* and accompanying memoir *Phantom Lobster*, in which lobsters represent the last chance 'for existence' for the small fishing community of Robin

Hood's Bay, which he calls Bramblewick. At that time the animal's inshore habitat of rocky ground was beyond the reach of destructive trawlers. The driving plot of *Phantom Lobster* is the author's invention of a folding iron trap that could be more easily transported and removed before heavy weather – to reduce the cost of lost and damaged traps, and in turn improve the livelihoods and safety of the men and their families. Walmsley's fishermen are proud, skilled, independent and laconic. They see lobsters in their traps as saviours and akin to riches. In *Phantom Lobster* a fisherman named Marney says: 'Lobsters are our only hope for making up what we lose on cod.'[14] In *Three Fevers* 'the market demand for lobsters was insatiable', and when the fishermen see an unexpected early 'blue-back' caught on a hook, it is 'as though it was a bar of gold from a sunken galleon'.[15] Marney

Herbert E. Butler's 1903 oil *Hauling in the Lobster Pot* depicts lobstermen off Polperro, Cornwall, as rugged, hard-working men out in the cold salt air; they are successful, too, considering the good catch already on board.

exclaims at one point: 'I tell you, lobsters are the best paying things in creation!'[16]

Back in New England, following the same trend, Louise Dickinson Rich also wrote about a lobster fishery reemerging as a viable business. In *The Peninsula* she portrays a small coastal fishing community in Corea, Maine. She describes her lobstermen even more effusively, reverentially. Unlike the men of Jewett's or Walmsley's towns, lobstering is now a sustainable year-round profession. Though the men use engines and motorized pot haulers, their work remains dangerous: 'The same ancient skills are necessary to lure the lobster to the trap . . . No labor law can be enacted that will dictate the turning of the tide, the path of a storm, or the crawling of the lobsters.'[17] For Rich a lobsterman represents an American ideal, 'pioneer stock', a self-reliant man making a living outside, similar perhaps to cultural images of the cowboy with 'an air and bearing of individual dignity that is almost regal'.[18] As to her lobsterman's perception of the animal, Rich wrote of an unloving pragmatism:

[Lobsters] are his living – these weird, grotesque creatures with their cunningly contrived and jointed plates of armor, their great, awkward claws, and their evil eyes looking out from the narrow green helmets. He removes them from the traps gingerly, grasping them about their bodies to avoid the viciously snapping claws and tails, and applies the metal rule that determines their legality.[19]

As the twentieth century wore on, more tourists, authors and artists visited the coast and, especially in the US, wrote more and more about these lobstermen, elevating the profession's image.[20] Nonfiction books such as *About Lobsters* (1962) and children's picture books such as *Lobsterman* (1962) added to the

A 1963 US Department of Commerce poster boosting travel in the United States shows the Maine lobsterman as a proud national symbol.

mystique. Painters such as Herbert E. Butler (*Hauling in the Lobster Pot*, 1903), Rockwell Kent (*Toilers of the Sea*, 1907) and N. C. Wyeth (*Deep Cove Lobster Man*, c. 1938) had painted solitary lobstermen working in difficult, romantic seascapes.

The lobster industry was similarly elevated in film in the twentieth century. In *It Happened to Jane* (1959), even a feisty New England lobster merchant, played by Doris Day, is celebrated. Rich's Corea was the subject of a documentary by French film-maker Jean Oser, titled *Lobstertown* (1947) and author E. B. White narrated another documentary titled *A Maine Lobsterman, or A Day in the Life of a Fisherman* (1954); both films reinforce the respect for this job. White says that the lobsterman is his own 'breed of men' who are 'born and not made'. Occasionally he speaks philosophically about how the sea is the lobsterman's ruling force, but the work provides 'a sense of freedom and assurance of hardihood that males unconsciously seek and need'.[21] White's patriotic admiration for this trade seemed to respond to a weariness with the world wars and a reaffirmation of individual liberties. He ends the film:

> [The lobsterboat] does not merely transport a man to his traps in the sea, it carries him in some degree to where all men want to go, toward the destination that gives the illusion of security and strength . . . [At the end of the day] the cove awaits him in tranquility. In lands where men are free, no sight is finer to the eye than a homecoming of an independent man, a trapper home from the sea.[22]

E. B. White saw lobstering as a solely masculine endeavour, but as early as the 1920s Arthur Train wrote a fictional story about a young woman hauling pots who is 'stalwart, erect, fearless . . . she was strong and brave and resourceful'.[23] And Louise Dickinson Rich described the first woman to hold a lobster licence in Maine, 'and that probably means in the world'.[24]

As far as I have found, the first fisherman to pen a major first-person narrative of the lobster fishery was Linda Greenlaw, who had spent over fifteen years as a deep-sea swordfisherman and captain, then took up lobstering. Her twenty-first-century *The Lobster Chronicles* does not wax poetic about blush-pink mornings on the water nor does she speak romantically of the immense skill of her fellow lobstermen, although she does say that they are independent and hard-working. She often says she hates lobstering, describing the gruelling, monotonous work.

At one point Greenlaw tells a story of the death of a fellow lobsterman, concluding: 'Death at sea is all a part of this life we have chosen, I sometimes think.'[25] Lobstering can indeed be

Linda Greenlaw, the first author of a significant first-person narrative about lobster fishing, here measures a lobster in Penobscot Bay, Maine, to determine if it is a legal 'keeper', c. 2002.

dangerous, especially when fishing alone, and because of the nature of most of lobster fisheries the work is often close to rocks and other navigational hazards. The greatest threat is from falling overboard in heavy weather or, in any conditions, getting your foot or arm caught in a line or trap that's whizzing over the side, tugging you down with it. Walmsley writes about a similar event in *Phantom Lobster*. A 1988 short story by John Hersey, 'The Captain', and a short-lived reality show *Lobstermen: Jeopardy at Sea* (2006) then *Lobster Wars* (2007), all set among the offshore lobstering fleet of New England, have amplified the dangers. In truth, however, as portrayed by Greenlaw, and as I can attest, most days lobstering, especially inshore, are more back-achingly monotonous than risky or hazardous.

In *The Lobster Chronicles* Greenlaw gives biological details about the lobster with a sense of humour: 'As far as I can see, there is absolutely nothing attractive about a lobster, male or female, and I have often wondered how so many manage to reproduce.'[26] Her perception of the animal aligns with other lobstermen as described by Jewett, Rich, White and Walmsley: the lobster for these fishermen is primarily a means to a livelihood. For several North American communities in the twenty-first century, lobstering is economically essential. Greenlaw reflects this: 'Other than the fact that we all live on this rock, our only common bond is lobster . . . Lobsters are tangible. Lobsters become the scapegoat, or perhaps it would be more accurate to say that all threats to our ability to catch lobsters become scapegoats.'[27]

Contemporary works of fiction have reinforced the idea of the lobsterman hero, but in stories such as 'The Captain', novels *Harbor Lights* (2000) and *The Wooden Nickel* (2002), and the movie *A Lobster Tale* (2006), these fishermen are more nuanced and human, their emotions and weaknesses exposed, their characters flawed. In Tim Winton's *Dirt Music* (2001), set on Australia's west coast, a highliner lobsterman finds 'the mother lode' in deep water. The man says: 'You asked if it was luck or brains. You know, right away, before we'd even finished pulling the first line I knew it was something else. It was too weird. Come noon, I was sure of it.'[28] He interprets the big catch of 'crays' as a sign and acts roughly, ineffectually, to rectify his past sins, including those against a local lobster poacher and his family.

One notable recent novel is *Stern Men* (2000) by Elizabeth Gilbert, in which the lobster industry dominates a fictional island community. Like Greenlaw, Gilbert does not romanticize her fishermen. She portrays them as fiercely competitive for territory and often backhanded and dishonest, although the men of the best lobstering family in the area are not only especially gifted fishermen but brave and Nordically handsome. In *Stern Men* Gilbert slips back and forth between anthropomorphizing the lobster – giving the animal human traits – and theriomorphizing people – giving them lobster-like traits, a narrative strategy used in nonfiction by Trevor Corson in *The Secret Life of Lobsters* (2004), in fiction by William Carpenter in *The Wooden Nickel*, and in a film by Todd Field and Rob Festinger titled *In the Bedroom* (2001). As *Stern Men*'s protagonist, island-born Ruth Thomas, transitions from adolescence to adulthood, the chapters' epigraphs feature quotations from lobster biology texts, such as Francis Herrick's, that match her own development. Once when Ruth visits her severely retarded brother she holds his hand and is reminded of a time when she was working aboard her father's boat, holding a newly moulted lobster:

The limp lobster hung on her hand, offering no more resistance than a wet sock . . . It was nothing like a normal lobster, nothing like one of those snappy fierce little tanks. And yet she could feel its life in her hand, its blood whirring in her palm. Its flesh was a bluish jelly, like a raw scallop . . . She had flung it over the side of the boat and watched it sink, translucent. It didn't have a chance. It didn't have a chance in the world. Something probably ate it before it even touched the bottom.[29]

Ruth thinks of lobsters more often, however, as ferocious survivors. She thinks that they'll be around for ever and could probably eat rocks if they had to. '*They don't give a shit*, Ruth thought, admiringly.'[30] At the start of the novel Gilbert introduces her lobstermen as fiercely territorial – they are not 'good neighbors' – because the animals they catch act as contentiously: 'Dairy farming makes men steady and reliable and temperate; deer hunting makes men quiet and fast and sensitive; lobster fishing makes men suspicious and wily and ruthless.'[31]

While some writers and artists have set the lobster underwater and more have focused on the lobsterman, still others have placed this animal on land as food on a plate or as a metaphor for a wide variety of emotions and ideas. Jack London, the writer better known for his animal stories of dogs and wolves, used the lobster as a symbol when he retold his own rendition of 'Pu-nia' within a short story 'The Water Baby' (1916). He probably heard 'Pu-nia' during his travels in Hawaii, and he was also probably aware of Kingsley's popular fairy tale *The Water-Babies*. London's 'The Water Baby' is the last story he wrote and critically recognized as one of his best.

At the end of 'The Water Baby' an old fisherman who has memorized many of the traditional Hawaiian songs and stories tells the tale of 'Pu-nia'. In this version, the community appeals to the boy, the Water Baby, because the king is coming and spiny lobster is his favourite food. 'And there were no lobsters, and it is not good to anger a king in the belly of him.'[32] Several men and women, old and young, have been eaten or maimed by the sharks, so they ask the child for help. The boy throws rocks to distract the sharks and returns with 'a fat lobster, a wahine lobster, full of eggs, for the king'.[33] The Water Baby turns the sharks on each other by saying the one with the shortest tail is the traitor. He simply does this over and over again, each time grabbing a fat lobster for the king, each time claiming the traitor is the one with the shortest tail. Finally the largest shark eats the second largest, and thus has eaten the equivalent of 39 other sharks. There is no Jonah-like ride inside the shark in London's version. The old storyteller says: 'And didn't they find the last shark on the beach next morning dead and burst wide open with all he had eaten?'[34] The Hawaiian tells the narrator this is a true story because he knows a relative of the Water Baby, he himself has dived for delicious lobsters over by the point, and he has seen 39 large lava rocks on the bottom.

In 'The Water Baby' London works overtly with the concept of the collective unconscious, the water as the place of birth, and the mystery and potential of dreams. His stories at the time were influenced by the writings of Carl Jung; he had been marking up a translation of *Psychology of the Unconscious* (1916), including the chapter 'Symbolism of Mother and Rebirth'.[35] In a Jungian interpretation of 'The Water Baby' literary scholar James McClintock sees the lobster as the 'treasure difficult of attainment'.[36]

Salvador Dalí's 1936 mixed media assemblage *Lobster Telephone* (also known as *Aphrodisiac Telephone*). Dalí wrote in 1948: 'I cannot understand why man should be capable of so little fantasy . . . when I ask for a grilled lobster in a restaurant, I am never served a cooked telephone.'

Jeff Koons, *Triple Elvis*, 2009, oil on canvas.

Where a Jungian might see a great deal in London's and Kingsley's connecting stories of water babies with the much-older tale of 'Pu-nia', a Freudian drools at the symbolic possibilities in this Hawaiian legend. A young boy's Oedipal fantasy is realized. After his father has been eaten by the dangerous foe, he emerges as the hero, providing delicious food for his mother, diving deep into the dark sea – a phallic manifest object in itself – and then provides red, sweet, salty food for his mother, equivalent in the child's mind to making love to her.

As discussed previously, lobster as a food is often used to evoke romance or lust. Authors and artists have extended this association well beyond the dining room. Salvador Dalí connected the lobster with sexuality, the unconscious and the surreal with his *Lobster Telephone* (1936), and Jeff Koons sexualized the lobster further, often replicating a lobster-shaped swimming pool float in his paintings and sculptures. Consider his *Triple Elvis* (2009), in which this lobster float, with antennae like Dalí's moustache, is painted across huge images of a nearly naked, buoyantly buxom Playboy model.[37] Referring to his polychromed aluminum sculpture of the pool toy, *Lobster*, which is hung suspended by a fat red chain, Koons said:

> I like the *Lobster* a lot because it's a symbol, both masculine and feminine. The tail tends to be very feminine, almost like a feather that a stripper might use in a performance.

Koons beside his 2004 sculpture *Lobster*. Is he doing a Dalí impression? Note the Dalíesque features of the lobster.

And the arms, the cross is more masculine. And the way the sculpture is painted, as the original inflatable was, it almost looks like fire, as if the lobster was burnt at the stake.[38]

No one has sought to connect human sexuality to lobsters as much as did French artist and author Guillaume Lecasble in his novella *Lobster* (2003), which I'm sure would have made Dalí proud. Lecasble's protagonist, Lobster, has an exceptional life. He 'had kept its animal instinct but his mind had been taken over by human thoughts'.[39] Lobster survives a boiling in a pot because just as he is thrown in, the ship he is aboard, the *Titanic*, sinks. As the vessel goes down he falls in love with the woman who had eaten his father, named Angelina. She soon learns that it is only Lobster who can give her a proper orgasm. (She tries later with another lobster with excruciatingly painful results.) All I will give away here is that the penis of a Parisian tattoo artist named Alfred eventually turns into a lobster. (If this novella is your cup of bisque, you may be obligated to rent the 1970 film *Multiple Maniacs*, in which a character named Divine is raped by a giant lobster.)

Authors and artists have used this animal for centuries to evoke the absurd and fantastic – and not always with an overt psychosexual charge. Anthropomorphized lobsters appear in a few nineteenth and twentieth-century fables, stories and poems,[40] but most famously in *Alice's Adventures in Wonderland* (1865). Lewis Carroll imagined 'The Lobster-Quadrille', a dance where lobsters are thrown as far as possible into the sea and then retrieved, and a poem "Tis the voice of the lobster' which comes out of Alice's mouth unexpectedly when she thinks she is going to be reciting 'The Sluggard', a real poem by Isaac Watts.[41] Alice recites:

George Platt Lynes, *Salvador Dalí*, 1939, gelatin silver print with applied pigment. Art historian Nancy Frazier wrote that for Dalí, a devoted student of Freud, the lobster represented both female penis envy and male fear of castration. See also Dalí's 1939 *The Dream of Venus* project.

William Heath, *The Prime Lobster*, 1828, hand-coloured engraving. A lobster was a derisive or comic term for a British soldier (think 'redcoat', for example). This cartoon depicts the former military hero Arthur Wellesley, Duke of Wellington, as a 'lobster' wearing the gown of the Chancellor of the Exchequer; George IV had appointed Wellington Prime Minister in 1828, causing some concern at the close involvement of the military in politics.

The PRIME *Lobster*

'Tis the voice of the Lobster: I heard him declare
'You have baked me too brown, I must sugar my hair.'
As a duck with its eyelids, so he with his nose
Trims his belt and his buttons, and turns out his toes.
When the sands are all dry, he is gay as a lark,
And will talk in contemptuous tones of the Shark:
But, when the tide rises and sharks are around,
His voice has a timid and tremulous sound.[42]

154

The lobster in literature has also been a tool to connote insanity. The author Théophile Gautier wrote about how his friend and colleague Gérard de Nerval walked a lobster through the streets of Paris:

'Why should a lobster be any more ridiculous than a dog?' [Nerval] used to ask quietly, 'or a cat, or a gazelle, or a lion, or any other animal that one chooses to take for a walk? I have a liking for lobsters. They are peaceful, serious creatures. They know the secrets of the sea, they don't bark, and they don't gnaw upon one's *monadic* privacy like dogs do. And Goethe had an aversion to dogs, and he wasn't mad.'[43]

John Tenniel's woodcut of 'Tis The Voice of the Lobster' for Lewis Carroll's *Alice's Adventures in Wonderland* (1865).

Nerval seems to have named his pet lobster 'Thibault', and at least one critic has seen this not as act of madness but a real effort to make his contemporaries question our claimed mastery of animals.[44] The poet Paul Muldoon references this pet in his poem 'Something Else' (1987) as a symbol of madness, referencing Nerval's suicide. In his novel *Pincher Martin* (1956), William Golding uses lobsters to highlight growing insanity, with the hallucinations of an island castaway:

> He eyed the peculiar shapes that lay across the trousers indifferently for a while until at last it occurred to him how strange it was that lobsters should sit there. Then he was suddenly seized with a terrible loathing for lobsters and flung them away so that they cracked on the rock. The dull pain of the blow extended him into them again and they became his hands, lying discarded where he had tossed them.[45]

Can I recommend just two more stories for your lobster library? One is by Samuel Beckett, the other by A. S. Byatt. File them under 'B' or on your shelf labelled 'Out of the Water Metaphors'. In Beckett's 1932 short story 'Dante and the Lobster' he used the animal as a Christ-like symbol, awaiting its death, and thus furthered ethical considerations about boiling these animals alive. The narrator, Belacqua, carries around a lobster from the fishmonger, unaware that it is still breathing. The animal is in a bag and is at one point pawed by a cat. On his way to visit his aunt, carrying the slowly dying lobster, the young man sees other things that make him think of euthanasia, pity, sacrifice and God's judgement. When he arrives at his aunt's house and goes down to her kitchen, 'into the bowels of the earth', she takes out the lobster, planning to cook it.

Belacqua says: 'Christ! it's alive,' and Beckett describes the lobster as an 'exposed cruciform'. As the aunt goes to put it in the pot, Belacqua is suddenly compassionate for the first time in the story: 'But it's not dead . . . you can't boil it like that.' The aunt replies: 'Have sense, lobsters are always boiled alive. They must be.' Though the animal 'trembled', the aunt tells him that 'they feel nothing'.[46] Beckett finishes the story:

> In the depths of the sea it had crept into the cruel pot. For hours, in the midst of its enemies, it had breathed secretly. It had survived the Frenchwoman's cat and his witless clutch. Now it was going alive into scalding water. It had to. Take into the air my quiet breath.
> . . .
> Well, thought, Belacqua, it's a quick death, God help us all. It is not.[47]

A. S. Byatt, who said Beckett's 'Dante and the Lobster' is 'one of the greatest short stories of all time', finished one of her own pieces, 'The Chinese Lobster' (1993), to emulate his, with similar imagery.[48] A lobster and two smaller crabs are slowly dying out of the water, on display, inside a Chinese restaurant. After an academic and a painter have a difficult lunch meeting about a suicidal graduate student, the two look at the dying animals on their way out. The crustaceans are 'still alive, all, more slowly, hissing their difficult air, bubbling, moving feet, feelers, glazing eyes'.[49] The academic, once suicidal herself, identifies with the dying animals, the 'pain of alien fish-flesh contracting inside an exo-skeleton'. Byatt writes as the story concludes:

> 'I find that *absolutely appalling*, you know', says Perry Diss [the painter]. 'And at the same time, exactly at the same

Felipe Dávalos drew lobsters as cute, relevant characters in Lee Wardlaw's version of the Hawaiian folktale *Punia and the King of Sharks* (1997).

time, I don't give a damn? D'you know?'
'I know,' says Gerda Himmelblau. She does know. Cruelly, imperfectly, voluptuously, clearly.[50]

Just as 'Pu·nia and the King of the Sharks' is still being performed by Hawaiian storytellers, has been retold and reworked in a story by Jack London and a modern children's book, so the descriptions, metaphors and characters created around the lobster have inspired the works of writers and artists. Mirroring societal views as well as helping to create them, our authors, filmmakers and painters have attached a wide variety of symbolism to lobsters, usually focusing on the animal's claws, its 'armour', its change of colour to a brilliant red after being cooked, and the fact that we regularly boil them alive – using these images to evoke unconscious desires, absurdity, pity or even madness. Some of our poets and musicians have been spiritually moved by the ability of lobster species to survive over the millennia under a dark, indifferent sea, while others, as evident in the B-52s's catchy pop song 'Rock Lobster' (1978), have had fun simply with the very sound, humour and versatility of the word. Like this: underwater like a mobster, lobster, lob to the surface, lobster and then, sadly, into the pot stir, lobster.

7 Feelers

The lobster has been variously praised and damned, copied
and rejected, romanticized and ridiculed. It has served as
fish bait, fertilizer, and gourmet food. It has appeared in
literary short stories, on license plates, and on tee shirts.
It has been envied and loved, steamed and boiled. But like
all true cultural icons . . . never been ignored.
George H. Lewis, 1998[1]

To consider our future relationship to the lobster, perhaps it's best that we embark on a Jules Verne zoom around the earth.

Let's start off tamely, beginning with the Florida Keys, and stop, gawk and laugh at 'Betsey', the giant spiny lobster sculpture beside the highway – one of several massive lobster totems that attract endless tourist cameras around the globe, from Shediac, New Brunswick, to Barcelona, Spain, to Kingston SE, South Australia.

Not far from Betsey, in a few areas within the Florida Keys National Marine Sanctuary, managers have had some success with reserves, at least in terms of rebuilding lobster populations. They have restricted or closed fishing entirely in these zones, yet still allowed lobstermen to set their traps outside the perimeters. Similarly regulated bodies of water are delineated off California and in the coastal waters of New Zealand, Belize, Brazil, Norway and the western Mediterranean. The Gulf of Mannar Biosphere Reserve off the coast of southeast India is the first marine reserve in southeast Asia, now protecting six species of spiny lobsters and one slipper species. These reserves might help both animals and fishermen in the long run, but the lobstermen of the Florida Keys are currently struggling because of a drop in the price of lobster due to the recession, and they are waiting to see how the BP oil spill of 2010 will affect future lobster stocks.

Let's next power through the Panama Canal, up the Pacific coast of Baja, and stop at Puerto Nuevo, Mexico. This tiny town holds an annual Fiesta de Langosta, featuring over thirty small restaurants sizzling up California spiny lobster by slicing them lengthwise, frying them in a pan with lard and serving them with rice, beans and flour tortillas. Puerto Nuevo calls itself the 'Lobster Capital of Baja'.[2]

Betsey, a giant spiny lobster sculpture in the Florida Keys, is just one of several monstrous lobster sculptures round the world.

Further north in the Monterey Bay Aquarium in Monterey, California, a 5 kg (11 lb) male spiny lobster sits passively between two rocks. A former big wave surfer named Tom Powers was free-diving off the Channel Islands:

I squirmed under the ledge and wrestled the bug out. In the meantime it had knocked my mask askew, completely flooding it, and had gotten a hold of my thumb with its

Tom Powers, a 6-foot-tall free diver, lost a piece of his glove to a California spiny lobster (*Panulirus interruptus*) before he was able to bring this 5 kg (11 lb) animal to the surface, 2009.

mandibles . . . it ended up taking the last couple inches off my Kevlar glove . . . I got back home and was on my way to the cleaning tables when I started to feel really bad about killing such a magnificent beast . . . I love to hunt and eat lobster, but giving this to the Aquarium was by far the most gratifying experience I've had in over ten years of hunting.[3]

Eleven pounds isn't nearly the size of the supposedly man-eating North Sea clawed lobsters as described in the sixteenth century, or even as large as those hefty ones recorded by early Europeans arriving at North America – but Powers's spiny bug is still an exceptionally large individual, even by historic standards in California.[4] The lobster lives in a tank that is small compared to what it is accustomed to, but this aquarium is a world leader in techniques for caring for marine animals and for advocating ocean conservation. When I visited, the aquarist in charge of this exhibit at the time, Kevin Lewand, sighed sympathetically. Yes, he told me, this animal probably would prefer a larger space, but if it lived in the huge kelp tank no one

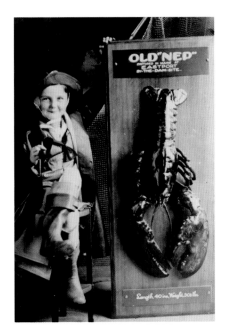

A child poses with Old 'Nep', c. 1930. This giant lobster, captured near Eastport, Maine, was 40 inches long and weighed 30 lb; it was displayed for many years at a local theatre.

would ever see it. Remember, lobsters are mostly nocturnal. 'This lobster is now an ambassador for his species', he said.[5] So the big lobster lives underneath a touch tank and is fed with meals delivered down on a skewer, a 'fish kebab'. Most people walk right past or don't notice as they play with the anemones or sea stars above. But every now and again someone kneels down and stares in awe at the lobster, or a volunteer points out the animal and describes its natural history and a bit about California marine reserves – highlighting the lobsters' role in the ecology of the kelp forest and how their populations impact the urchins and sea otters.

If there are broad themes to be taken from this lobster study, one is that giant individuals fascinate us. They evoke an earlier

Utagawa
Kuniyoshi
(1798–1861),
'Phoenix and
Lobster', from
the *Birds and
Animals Illustrated*
series, late 1830s,
woodblock print.

earth: less spoiled but more threatening. As we now travel across the North Pacific, recall the scene in *Twenty Thousand Leagues under the Sea* (1869) where enormous crustaceans crawl along the ocean floor. Professor Aronnax describes an encounter:

> My blood curdled when I saw enormous antennae block-ing my road, or some frightful claw closing with a noise in the shadow of some cavity. Millions of luminous spots shone brightly amid the shadows. They were the eyes of giant crustacea crouched in their lairs; giant lobsters setting themselves up like halberdiers, and moving their claws with the clicking sound of pincers.[6]

A large lobster is a survivor among a group of animals who are survivors, whose ancestors foraged the sea for tens of millions of years before *Homo sapiens* appeared. Francis Herrick wrote in his *Natural History of the American Lobster*:

> Giants are met with in all the higher groups of animals. They interest us not only on account of their actual size, but also in showing to what degree individuals may sur-pass the mean average of the race. It may be a question whether lobsters weighing from 20 to 30 pounds [9–14 kg] or more are to be regarded as giants in the technical sense, or simply as sound and vigorous individuals on whose side fortune has always fought in the struggle for life. I am inclined to the latter view, and look upon the mammoth lobster simply as a favorite of nature, who is larger than his fellows because he is their senior; good luck never deserted him until he was stranded on the beach or became entangled in some fisherman's gear.[7]

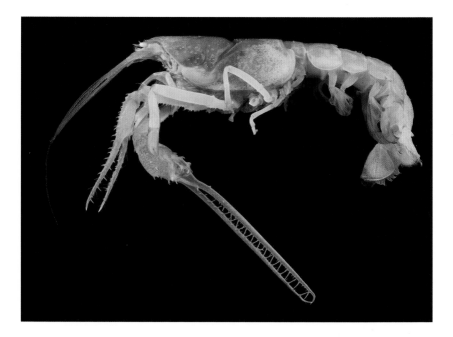

This newly discovered blind lobster, named *Dinochelus* (meaning 'terrible claw') *ausubeli* in 2010, was captured in depths of about 300 metres (980 feet) near the Philippines.

One of the brasher volunteers at the aquarium declared that Powers's spiny lobster is 80 to 90 years old, but we can't be sure of the age of any large lobster. Because they so completely shed their shell, nothing remains that can be dated, nothing like the otoliths with growth rings found inside a fish's head. Biologists believe lobsters moult once every year or two, but the rate of shedding and the amount they expand seems to diminish as they age and is subject to environmental conditions. Scientists have created size estimates, predicted-growth curves, but nothing is certain since so few of these specimens have lived in captivity for decades. Promising new methods for ageing crustaceans use a pigment, lipofuscin, sampled from the cells of lobster nervous systems – but these are not yet reliable.[8]

Based on its size, it is safer to say Powers's spiny catch is 30 to 40 years old.[9]

Returning to our lobster-centric, Verne-style circumnavigation, we continue along the surface of the North Pacific off Japan, where float the extraordinary transparent phyllosoma of spiny and slipper lobsters. In the deep black water, some 180 metres (600 feet) down, scuttle specimens of *Thaumastocheles japonicus*, little lobsters with one claw exceptionally longer and toothier than the other. These bizarre lobsters are barely known to science – described only from a few rare specimens that appeared like pale space creatures aboard a fishing or research vessel. New species, new genera even, have turned up in recent years.[10]

If there is a second broader theme to this lobster study, it is that the definition of a lobster continues to evolve and spur debate, in part because of advanced technologies, but also because the ocean is an enormous, inaccessible place: we keep finding new crustaceans. In 2010 lobster taxonomist Tin-Yam Chan of National Taiwan Ocean University published a brand new master list of lobsters, differing from Holthuis and others in a variety of ways, incorporating the most advanced phylogenetics and recent discoveries. He counted '248 valid species (with four valid subspecies) of marine lobsters in 6 families and 55 genera'.[11]

At the diverse fish markets of China and Japan, well before dawn most days, several lobster species arrive both live and frozen from all over the world, often as by-catch from other fisheries. In the larger cities, such as Hong Kong, Beijing, Taipei and Tokyo, restaurants have been serving more 'Maine' lobster, while varieties of spiny and slipper lobsters have been prepared in Asian kitchens for centuries. The bright red or orange colour is particularly appreciated for special occasions, evoking celebration and wealth.

For the aquarium trade, divers gather the little Hawaiian reef lobster, *Enoplometopus occidentalis,* from waters throughout the tropical Indo-Pacific.

To supply the international demand for lobsters, aquaculture producers, fisheries managers and scientists in, for instance, Australia, India and Norway, have been developing all manner of aquaculture, mariculture and sea ranching methods to raise lobsters at various developmental stages. Some raise lobster larvae from eggs in the laboratory then release these into the wild. Others collect larvae and raise individuals in tanks. Artificial habitats are placed in the ocean to increase survivability of larvae while adult lobsters are moved from one part of the sea to another in hopes they will grow faster and healthier. Vietnamese aquaculturists, for example, collect spiny lobster post-larvae from the ocean, a portion in shipments from Bangladesh, and then grow them out to adults in tanks or cages, exporting more than 1,000 tonnes to markets throughout Asia. Scientists have been researching lobster aquaculture methods since before

Francis Herrick's day – usually without enough success to make it commercially viable or quantifiably helpful to local fisheries.[12] The twenty-first century should continue to see significant advances here, although most of the lobster aquaculture research, involving over ten different lobster species, is closely guarded since the profit potential is enormous.[13]

In southeast Asia, in Indonesian waters, locals catch finger-sized, magnificently coloured lobsters for the aquarium trade, known generally in the industry as purple or red lobsters (*Enoplometopus sp.*), and whose taxonomy is still debated. Novice aquarium enthusiasts halfway across the world like the idea of a pretty little lobster in their tank – yet often wake up to find their new pet has eaten a few of their prized tropical fish.[14]

We'll next sail to Fremantle Harbour, Western Australia. Here the guests of Cicerello's, a popular restaurant here since the 1940s, relax outside, watch the vessels go in and out of the port and look across the harbour at a heroic bronze sculpture:

Greg James's 2004 bronze sculpture *The Fishermen* is an extensive project installed at the harbour of Fremantle, Western Australia. Fishing for 'crays', the lobsterman depicted here works both a historic 'beehive pot' and a contemporary 'slatty pot'.

a man lifting a lobster trap. The customers can watch their lobsters in the tank before the animals are prepared for dinner, which at Cicerello's is usually split, grilled and simply basted with garlic butter, then served with a sprinkling of parsley. Henry Liascos, the owner, told me this story:

> Once two idiots, drunk, came in and stole out of our aquarium the largest cray we had, in full view of our customers, who called me and pointed to the direction the culprits went, into the park and across the road. I gave chase and found one of the idiots trying to hide it by wedging it between his butt and the base of a tree. I pushed him off-balance, grabbed the cray, and ran back to the shop. As I arrived I was greeted by the diners with a cheer. One lady said: 'Yeah! One for the good guys!'[15]

We're off across the Indian Ocean, pausing to observe the Blunt slipper lobster (*Scyllarides squammosus*) off Madagascar, one of the largest, most cosmopolitan and tastiest of the slippers, found in waters as distant as Japan, Australia and Hawaii. In more distant waters nearly 500 miles south of Madagascar, South African scientists in 2006 discovered an entirely new species of lobster, *Palinurus barbarae*, living on a submerged seamount. These remote giants weighed up to 4 kg (8.8 lb).

We now navigate north, through the Suez Canal, to look at a few of the Mediterranean lobsters, the animals which the Hebrews denied themselves because they perceived them as unclean, as scavengers, and the same species once enjoyed by the Greeks and Romans.

Across Europe, across Italy and Spain – two of the larger importers of American lobster[16] – then we touch down in London to visit the office of the Marine Stewardship Council.

MSC runs an 'ecolabel' programme to inform consumers about environmentally sustainable fisheries. They've given their certification to the spiny lobster industry off Western Australia (2000/2006), the first of *any* fishery in the world, and that of Mexican Baja California (2004), a small collection of some 500 lobstermen organised in nine cooperatives. In 2010 the Canadian offshore lobster fishery earned certification. This fishery is run by one company, owning all of the licences, operating year-round under a seemingly sustainable total allowable catch.[17] Together the lobstermen of Jersey and Normandy have begun the expensive MSC certification process.[18]

Conservation biologists, such as Daniel Pauly at the University of British Columbia and Callum Roberts at the University of York, see the growth of invertebrate fisheries as alarming, regardless of how careful we are about the methods. They believe we are 'fishing down marine food webs', reducing diversity and increasing species' vulnerability to disease – as exemplified by the 'shell-rot' disease on the lobsters in John Whittaker's southern New England, or the *Haematodinium* parasite, which has infected pockets of the Norway lobster, *Nephrops norvegicus*.[19] Roberts writes:

> One widespread change has been the shift from finfish to invertebrate dominance. The switch from cod to crab, lobster, and prawns in Canada; the flip from groundfish to lobster and urchins in the Gulf of Maine; the rise of *Nephrops* prawns in northern Europe as their fish predators diminish. This invertebrate ascendancy is welcomed by fishers, for their flesh is valuable, sometimes more so than the fish they replaced. But there is grave risk in our uncontrolled experiments with nature.[20]

Cruising outbound along the Thames, where once sailing vessels with wells delivered live lobsters to Billingsgate Market, we travel north until we're off the coast of Fife. Here the *Nephrops* fishery continues to be one of the remaining money-makers, while the European lobster is making a comeback according to Ian Murray, a retired skipper and wholesaler, who told me that 2009 was 'the best ever for lobsters, not just in the St Andrews area but right up and down the whole East Coast'.[21]

Now across our last ocean, the Atlantic, and into the waters of the Gulf of Maine where you should mull over a recent study by researchers who used underwater cameras to reveal that American lobsters are actually more capable of climbing out of traps than previously thought. This suggests perhaps it is just as much timing that catches the bugs after all.[22]

In truth, biologists and fishermen still do not have a complete understanding of the whys and wheres of adult lobster movement or larval settlement. There remains an extraordinary amount that we still do not know, even about American lobsters, arguably the most studied marine animal on earth. To mark the first edition of Herrick's seminal book, then titled *The American Lobster: A Study of Its Habits and Developments* (1895), another entire text was devoted to the study of this animal, edited by Jan Factor, this time written by more than a dozen specialists and called simply *Biology of the Lobster 'Homarus americanus'* (1995).

Behold the future of the global lobster industry at the Ocean Choice processing plant in Souris, Prince Edward Island, Canada. Ocean Choice purchases hundreds of thousands of pounds of *Homarus americanus* from Canadian and American fishermen each year. Ocean Choice ships the lobsters, which they dub 'the king of seafood', around the world in various forms, organized through their offices in the US, the UK, Germany, Japan and China. They'll ship ready-for-retail whole lobsters in a bag that

An Ocean Choice International wholesale brochure exemplifies the variety of lobster products offered by a 21st-century Canadian lobster processor using advanced hyperbaric and freezing technologies.

has been quick-frozen. They offer a dizzying variety of lobster meat – tails, claws, knuckles – that a store can sell frozen, cooked or canned. Ocean Choice also has the machinery to take live lobsters through a water-filled pressure chamber. This 'hyperbaric process' allows the meat to slip right out of the shell with little effort, to be sold as frozen, shell-free refrigerated parts, similar to how you would buy boned chicken breast at the supermarket.[23]

A fledgling processing company in Maine, which has also invested in this hyperbaric machinery, sells frozen bags of 'Maine Lobster Spaghetti', full of the thin strips of leg meat that are difficult to extract if you're eating the bugs in the rough.[24] Meanwhile, anticipating ever-increasing twenty-first-century regulations intended to protect animal welfare and perhaps a

A chef about to kill a lobster with Crustastun's 'single stunner'. The company claims that the electric current stops the functioning of the lobster's nervous system in less than half a second so that the animal can't feel pain as the current continues, rendering the lobster 'brain dead' within five seconds.

growing public response to claims that crustaceans feel pain, an English company has manufactured 'Crustastun', a device that zaps the lobster with 'an instant current', killing it in seconds.[25] The company offers an industrial conveyor belt model and a personal, scanner-sized device for restaurants: 'the single stunner'.

A solitary European lobster in the Outer Hebrides. In the words of the Scottish poet George Mackay Brown in his 'Lobster': 'The orchards where you wander/Drop sufficient plunder,/Mercenary in the dark blue coat of mail'.

This growing public empathy for the lobster as a sentient animal evokes a third larger lesson from this lobster study: our cultural relationships with this animal as a food and as a symbol are extraordinarily varied and at times completely contradictory. We anthropomorphize the lobster, but it is one of the few animals we still kill in our homes. We claim it is an aphrodisiac, but we use the animal for absurdist comedy and costumes, then, around the next corner, association with the lobster is a metaphor for madness.

We'll end this world lobster tour in New York City, where the earliest commercial lobstermen of the US, many from Whittaker's Noank, Connecticut, once sold their catch.

One final story. After a long day of lobster study in Manhattan, I went into the bar at City Crab and Seafood for refreshment. Making conversation, and perhaps because I did not look urban enough, the bartender asked when I sat down: 'Been in the Big Apple long?'

'Just came in this morning', I said.

On the way from the library I had stopped to see a Red Lobster, one of their nearly 700 restaurants across North America. On a corner amidst the lights of Times Square, this Red Lobster is appropriately in the theatre district where the lobster palaces once flourished in the early 1900s. Just above their front door, the restaurant has a large Jeff Koonsian lobster, revolving and red-lit.

I wanted to sit down at City Crab and Seafood, though, to see the plaque just above their tank filled with live Dungeness crabs and American lobsters. It says:

Good Luck, George!
City Crab and Seafood Company

George the Lobster
Our beloved 20 lb 140-year-old unofficial mascot
has been returned to the sea.
January 9, 2009

General manager Mitchell Rosen explained to me that one afternoon they had a big lobster in the tank and two women came into the bar. They asked about it. The next day City Crab received a call from PETA. City Crab was happy to release the animal. The big bug would have been harder to sell and prepare, and it got the restaurant all sorts of positive press. Rosen said he received over 400 emails from all over the world. He conceded he has no idea if the lobster is 140 years old, but that's what *somebody* said.[26] This is not an isolated event. People have been releasing (and naming) large individual lobsters for decades, and celebrities such as Mary Tyler Moore, Ellen DeGeneres and Paul McCartney have for just as long advocated lobster rights. Not bad for a prickly underwater bug.

When my drink arrived, at last, I raised my glass to the plaque: Good luck, lobster. Be content, be content far out.

Timeline of the Lobster

250 MYA (PERMO-TRIASSIC)

The clawed and spiny lobster evolutionary tracks diverge, with major differences today evident in larval development, habitat, and structure of front legs and antennae

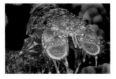

150 MYA (MID-JURASSIC)

The large clawed lobsters exist in a similar form to that we recognize today, and perhaps less than 2.5 MYA (Pleistocene) they begin to evolve into separate species (*Homarus americanus* and *H. gammarus*) with different ranges on either side of the North Atlantic Ocean

c. 1495 BCE

Probably the earliest known depiction of a lobster is a carving on a temple's wall in Deir el-Bahri, recording an Egyptian voyage to the Red Sea

c. 1660

The first known commercial export lobster fishery begins as Dutch ships sail regularly to buy lobster from Norwegian fishermen

1770

Joseph Banks describes spiny lobsters as a plentiful luxury food for the ship, caught off the coast of New Zealand by Maoris, who find the animals with their feet

1840s–1900

Canning technology expands markets for lobster meat and sparks a Lobster Rush in North America, severely depleting lobster stocks in the Gulfs of Maine and St Lawrence

1895

Francis Hobart Herrick writes *The American Lobster: Its Habits and Development*, revised as *Natural History of the American Lobster* in 1911

1954

E. B. White's narration of the documentary film *A Maine Lobsterman* contributes to an emerging cultural perception of the lobster fisherman as an independent hard-working hero

1986

George Mackay Brown publishes his poem 'Lobster'

c. 1980s

Lobster landings in Atlantic Canada and the Gulf of Maine begin to rise until they double, then triple previous catches

1990s

Shell disease, die-offs and a major oil spill off Rhode Island severely diminish the lobster fishery of Long Island Sound and southern New England

c. 350 BCE	1555	1620	1634

In *Historia Animalium* Aristotle includes careful and mostly accurate biological descriptions of clawed and spiny lobsters

An image in *Historia de Gentibus Septentrionalibus* by Olaus Magnus depicts a giant lobster snatching a man off a ship

Dr Tobias Venner, in his *Via Recta ad Vitam Longam*, believes lobster to be an aphrodisiac, warning that this shellfish 'maketh a great propensitie unto venereall embracements'

William Wood describes American lobsters as huge, plentiful, 'luscious', but also 'seldom eaten', and he writes that Native Americans use lobsters for bait and dry the lobsters on scaffolds to eat later in the year

c. 1900	c. 1900–1920	1932	1936

The development of the internal combustion engine ushers in a series of technological advances in catching lobsters around the world, notably the use of plastics, the wire trap, radar, scuba and GPS – the introduction of freezing technologies and airline shipping later this century will further expand markets worldwide

Decadent, scandalous, late-night restaurants, called 'lobster palaces' are popular in New York City for the rich and famous

Leo Walmsley publishes *Three Fevers* then *Phantom Lobster* the following year, elevating societal respect for the profession of lobster fishing

Salvador Dalí's creates his mixed-media sculpture *Lobster Telephone*, evoking cultural attitudes of the lobster as both an absurd and sexual symbol

2000	2002	2010	2011

The Western rock lobster fishery (*Panulirus cygnus*), the largest and most valuable single-species catch in Australia, is the first fishery of any kind to be certified for sustainability by the Marine Stewardship Council

In *The Lobster Chronicles: Life on a Very Small Island* Linda Greenlaw writes the first major first-person narrative of life as a lobster fisherman

Scientists continue to struggle with the taxonomy of lobsters and what actually is a lobster, as evident with the publication 'Annotated Checklist of the World's Marine Lobsters' by Taiwanese biologist Tin-Yam Chan

Lobstermen struggle due to the fall of the global economy: a reminder that lobster remains a luxury food – climate change, urban pollution, new fisheries management strategies and developments in aquaculture will all affect lobster populations in the future

References

1 WHAT IS A LOBSTER?

1 W. B. Lord, *Crab, Shrimp, and Lobster Lore* (London, 1867), p. 96.
2 James M. Acheson, *Capturing the Commons: Devising Institutions to Manage the Maine Lobster Industry* (Hanover, NH, 2003), p. 206.
3 John Steinbeck, *Travels with Charley: In Search of America* (New York, 1963), pp. 48–9.
4 L. B. Holthuis, FAO *Species Catalogue: Volume 13, Marine Lobsters of the World: An Annotated and Illustrated Catalogue of Species of Interest to Fisheries Known to Date* (Rome, 1991), p. 8; FAO, *Fisheries and Aquaculture Statistics, 2006* (Rome, 2008), p. 52; 'Commercial Fishery Landings: Seafisheries', *Fisheries and Oceans Canada*, available at www.dfo-mpo.gc.ca, accessed 24 August 2010; Elizabeth S. Pritchard, ed., National Marine Fisheries Service, Office of Science and Technology, *Fisheries of the United States 2008* (Silver Spring, MD, 2009), p. 3.
5 Thuy Pham and Alistair Peat, Australian Bureau of Agricultural and Resource Economics, 'Australian Fisheries Statistics 2008' (Canberra, 2009), p. 65; Kasia Mazur et al., Australian Bureau of Agricultural and Resource Economics, 'Australian Fisheries – The Global Context', *Issues Insights 10.3* (Canberra, 2010), p. 11.
6 National Marine Fisheries statisics 2003 in Alice Cascorbi, 'Seafood Watch Seafood Report: Spiny Lobsters Vol. II', *Monterey Bay Aquarium Update* (10 February 2004), p. 7.
7 Aristotle, 'History of Animals', trans. D'Arcy Wentworth Thompson, *The Complete Works of Aristotle*, ed. Jonathan Barnes (Princeton, NJ, 1985), vol. I, bk. IV, p. 833.

8 A.S.D. Farmer, 'Synopsis of Biological Data on the Norway Lobster, *Nephrops norvegicus* (Linnaeus, 1758)', *FAO Fisheries Synopsis No. 112* (Rome, 1975), p. 3.

9 L. B. Holthuis, *Marine Lobsters of the World* (2006) (an update of his 1991 FAO report, launched by the World Biodiversity Database) available at nlbif.eti.uva.nl/bis/lobsters.php, accessed 24 August 2010.

10 'Lobster', *Oxford English Dictionary*, 2nd edn (Oxford, 1989).

11 J. Stanley Cobb and Bruce F. Phillips, *The Biology and Management of Lobsters* (London, 1980), vol. I, pp. xi; B. F. Phillips, J. S. Cobb and B. W. George, 'General Biology', ibid., p. 12.

12 Phillips, Cobb and George, 'General Biology', p. 7.

13 Holthuis, *FAO Species Catalogue*, vol. 13, p. 167.

2 DISSECTING A BUG

1 Ralph Waldo Emerson, 'The Uses of Natural History', in *Reading the Roots: American Nature Writing before 'Walden'*, ed. Michael P. Branch (Athens, GA, 2004), p. 278.

2 This interview and dissection with Dr Jonathan Geller was conducted on 16 July 2009 at the Moss Landing Marine Laboratories, California State University.

3 S. L. Waddy, D. E. Aiken and D.P.V. de Kleijn, 'Control of Growth and Reproduction' in *Biology of the Lobster 'Homarus americanus'*, ed. Jan Robert Factor (London, 1995), p. 258.

4 Michael J. Childress and Steven H. Jury, 'Behaviour', in *Lobsters: Biology, Management, Aquaculture and Fisheries*, ed. Bruce F. Phillips (Oxford, 2006), pp. 81–3.

5 William Herrnkind, 'Queuing Behavior of Spiny Lobsters', *Science*, CLXIV/3886 (20 June 1969), p. 1425; and 'Strange March of the Spiny Lobster', *National Geographic*, CXLVII/6 (June 1975), pp. 819, 829.

6 K. L. Lavalli and J. R. Factor, 'The Feeding Appendages', in *Biology of the Lobster 'Homarus americanus'*, ed. Jan Robert Factor (London, 1995), pp. 383, 389.

7 J. Atema and R. Voigt, 'Behavior and Sensory Biology', in *Biology of the Lobster 'Homarus americanus'*, ed. Jan Robert Factor (London, 1995), p. 341.

8 Trevor Corson, *The Secret Life of Lobsters: How Fishermen and Scientists Are Unraveling the Mysteries of Our Favorite Crustacean* (New York, 2005), p. 189.

9 B. F. Phillips, J. S. Cobb and R. W. George, 'General Biology', in *The Biology and Management of Lobsters*, ed. J. Stanley Cobb and Bruce F. Phillips (London, 1980), vol. I, pp. 26–7; Childress and Jury, 'Behaviour', p. 83.

10 Waddy, Aiken and de Kleijn, 'Control of Growth and Reproduction', p. 258.

11 Larry C. Boles and Kenneth J. Lohmann, 'True Navigation and Magnetic Maps in Spiny Lobsters', *Nature*, CDXXI (2 January 2003), pp. 60–63.

12 Childress and Jury, 'Behaviour', p. 82.

13 Phillips, Cobb and George, 'General Biology', pp. 22–4.

14 Waldo L. Schmitt, *Crustaceans* (Ann Arbor, MI, 1965), p. 154.

15 William Eddis, *Letters from America, Historical and Descriptive* (London, 1792), pp. 426–7; see also Erich Pontoppidan, *Natural History of Norway, Part II* (London, 1755), p. 173.

16 For example, T. M. Prudden, *About Lobsters* (Freeport, ME, 1982), p. 19.

17 Childress and Jury, 'Behaviour', p. 78.

18 J. S. Cobb and K. M. Castro, '*Homarus* Species', in *Lobsters: Biology, Management, Aquaculture and Fisheries*, ed. Bruce F. Phillips (Oxford, 2006), p. 310.

19 Diane Cowan, 'A Lobster of a Different Color', *Commercial Fisheries News* (January 2000), p. 14A.

20 Phillips, Cobb and George, 'General Biology', pp. 20–21.

21 W. B. Lord, *Crab, Shrimp, and Lobster Lore* (London, 1867), p. 105.

22 C. K. Govind, 'Muscles and their Innervation', in *Biology of the Lobster 'Homarus americanus'*, ed. Jan Robert Factor (London, 1995), p. 298.

23 Phillips, Cobb and George, 'General Biology', p. 20.

24 Atema and Voigt, 'Behavior and Sensory Biology', p. 316.

25 Francis Hobart Herrick, *Natural History of the American Lobster* (Washington, DC, 1911), p. 253.

26 Stanley Cobb, personal communication, 14 November 2009, Kingston, Rhode Island.

27 G. O. Sars, 'Reports Made to the Department of the Interior of Investigations of the Salt-water Fisheries of Norway during the Years 1874–77', trans. Herman Jacobson, *United States Commission of Fish and Fisheries: Report of the Commissioner for 1877*, pt. V (Washington, DC, 1879), p. 677.

28 Waddy, Aiken and de Kleijn, 'Control of Growth and Reproduction', pp. 220–21.

29 Cobb, personal communication, 14 November 2009.

30 R. C. O'Farrell, *Lobsters, Crabs and Crawfish* (London, 1966), p. 20.

31 C. F. Chubb and E. H. Barker, *The Western Rock Lobster Fishery 1995/6 to 1996/7*, Fisheries Research Report no. 135 (North Beach, WA, 2002), pp. 11–12.

32 Herrick, *Natural History of the American Lobster*, p. 188.

33 T. H. Huxley, *The Crayfish: An Introduction to the Study of Zoology* (London, 1977 [1880]), p. 13; Axel Boeck, 'The Norwegian Lobster-Fishery and Its History', *United States Commission of Fish and Fisheries, Report of the Commissioner for 1873–4 and 1874–5*, pt. III ed. Spencer F. Baird (Washington, DC, 1876), p. 223.

34 Jean de La Fontaine, *The Fables of La Fontaine*, trans. Elizur White (London, 1888), p. 319.

35 Jasper White, *Lobster at Home* (New York, 1998), p. 17.

36 Herrick, *Natural History of the American Lobster*, p. 249.

37 Barbara Beltz, 'Neurobiology and Neuroendocrinology', in *Biology of the Lobster 'Homarus americanus'*, ed. Jan Robert Factor (London, 1995), p. 268.

38 Corson, *The Secret Life of Lobsters*, p. 196.

39 White, *Lobster at Home*, p. 20.

40 Herrick, *Natural History of the American Lobster*, pp. 289–97; D. E. Aiken and S. L. Waddy, 'Reproductive Biology', in *The Biology and*

Management of Lobsters, ed. J. Stanley Cobb and Bruce F. Phillips (London, 1980), vol. I, pp. 259–60.

41 Herrick, *Natural History of the American Lobster*, p. 319.

42 Ibid., p. 298.

43 Phillips, Cobb and George, 'General Biology', p. 55.

44 B. F. Phillips, P. A. Brown, D. W. Rimmer and D. D. Reid, 'Distribution and Dispersal of the Phyllosoma Larvae of the Western Rock Lobster, *Panulirus cygnus*, in the South-eastern Indian Ocean', *Australian Journal of Marine and Freshwater Research*, XXX/6 (1979), p. 781.

45 B. F. Phillips, J. D. Booth, J. S. Cobb, A. G. Jeffs and P. McWilliam, 'Larval and Postlarval Ecology', in *Lobsters: Biology, Management, Aquaculture and Fisheries*, ed. Bruce F. Phillips (Oxford, 2006), p. 234.

46 Phillips, Cobb and George, 'General Biology', pp. 5–6.

3 ANCIENT, GIANT AND PLENTIFUL

1 Axel Boeck, 'The Norwegian Lobster-Fishery and Its History,' *United States Commission of Fish and Fisheries, Report of the Commissioner for 1873–4 and 1874–4*, pt. III, ed. Spencer F. Baird (Washington, DC, 1876), pp. 223–4.

2 George Bruce, *Wrecks and Reminiscences of St Andrews Bay* (Dundee, 1884), pp. 13–20.

3 Neil Cameron, 'St Rule's Church, St Andrews, and Early Stone-Built Churches in Scotland', *Proceedings of the Society of Antiquaries of Scotland*, CXXIV (1994), p. 367.

4 Bruce, *Wrecks and Reminiscences of St Andrews Bay*, p. 30.

5 James R. Coull, 'Shellfishing', in *Scottish Life and Society: Boats, Fishing and the Sea*, ed. James R. Coull, Alexander Fenton and Kenneth Veitch (Edinburgh, 2008), vol. IV, p. 375.

6 Ibid.

7 Bruce J. Bourque, *Twelve Thousand Years: American Indians in Maine* (London, 2001), p. 85.

8 Antonieta Jerardino and René Navarro, 'Cape Rock Lobster (*Jasus*

lalandii) Remains from South African West Coast Shell Middens: Preservational Factors and Possible Bias', *Journal of Archaeological Science*, xxix (2002), pp. 993–4; Robert J. Losey, Sylvia Behrens Yamada and Leah Largaespada, 'Late-Holocene Dungeness Crab (*Cancer magister*) Harvest at an Oregon Coast Estuary', *Journal of Archaeological Science*, xxxi (2004), pp. 1603, 1605.

9 John R. Grindley, 'The Cape Rock Lobster *Jasus lalandii* from the Bonteberg Excavation', *South African Archaeological Bulletin*, xxii/87 (November 1967), p. 94; B. F. Leach, 'Fish and Crayfish from the Washpool Midden Site, New Zealand: Their Use in Determining Season of Occupation and Prehistoric Fishing Methods', *Journal of Archaeological Science*, vi/2 (1979), pp. 111, 120–21.

10 Nicolas Baudin, *The Journal of Post Captain Nicolas Baudin*, trans. Christine Cornell (Adelaide, 1974), p. 350.

11 Willy Ley, *Dawn of Zoology* (Englewood Cliffs, NJ, 1968), p. 10.

12 Elizabeth P. Benson, *Birds and Beasts of Ancient Latin America* (Gainesville, FL, 1997), p. 120; Robert Blakey, *Old Faces in New Masks* (London, 1859), pp. 370–71; Waldo L. Schmitt, *Crustaceans* (Ann Arbor, MI, 1965), p. 15.

13 Blakey, *Old Faces in New Masks*, p. 362.

14 Pliny the Elder, *The Natural History of Pliny*, trans. John Bostock and H. T. Riley (London, 1890), vol. ii, n. 61, p. 423.

15 Blakey, *Old Faces in New Masks*, pp. 361–2.

16 Pliny the Elder, *The Natural History of Pliny*, p. 360.

17 Ley, *Dawn of Zoology*, p. 116; Olaus Magnus, *Historia de Gentibus Septentrionalibus* (*Descriptions of the Northern Peoples*, 1555) (London, 1998), vol. iii, bk. 21, ch. 34, p. 1118.

18 Erich Pontoppidan, *Natural History of Norway, Part ii* (London, 1755), p. 172.

19 John Josselyn, *John Josselyn, Colonial Traveler: A Critical Edition of 'Two Voyages to New-England'*, ed. Paul J. Lindholdt (London, 1988), p. 79; William Wood, *New England's Prospect*, ed. Alden T. Vaughan (Amherst, MA, 1993), p. 56.

20 Reverend Francis Higginson, *New-Englands Plantation with The*

Sea Journal and Other Writings (Salem, MA, 1908), pp. 88, 97.

21 Francis Hobart Herrick, *Natural History of the American Lobster* (Washington, DC, 1911), p. 195.

22 'King of All the Lobsters', *The New York Times* (20 March 1897), available at www.nytimes.com, accessed 24 August 2010.

23 Norris McWhirter et al., eds, *Guinness Book of World Records 1985* (New York, 1984), p. 68.

24 John Major, *A History of Greater Britain as well England as Scotland*, trans. and ed. Archibald Constable (Edinburgh, 1892), pp. 33–4.

25 Anthony Parckhurst, 'A letter written to M. Richard Hakluyt of the middle Temple, conteining [sic] a report of the true state and commodities of Newfoundland', in *The Principal Navigations, Voyages, Traffiques, and Discoveries of the English Nation*, ed. Richard Hakluyt (Glasgow, 1904), vol. XIII, p. 12.

26 'The Voyage of M. Charles Leigh', in *The Principal Navigations, Voyages, Traffiques, and Discoveries of the English Nation*, ed. Richard Hakluyt (Glasgow, 1904), vol. XIII, p. 174.

27 Henry O. Thayer, *The Sagadahoc Colony, comprising The Relation of a Voyage into New England* (Portland, ME, 1892), p. 45.

28 James Rosier, *Rosier's Relation of Waymouth's Voyage to the Coast of Maine, 1605*, ed. Henry S. Burrage (Portland, ME, 1887), p. 104.

29 John Smith, *A Description of New England; or, Observations and Discoveries in the North of America in the Year of our Lord 1614* (Boston, 1865), p. 48.

30 Thomas Morton, *New English Canaan*, ed. Jack Dempsey (Scituate, MA, 2000), p. 87.

31 Marc Lescarbot, *The History of New France*, trans. and ed. W. L. Grant (Toronto, 1914), vol. III, p. 238.

32 Rosier, *Rosier's Relation of Waymouth's Voyage*, p. 124.

33 Morton, *New English Canaan*, p. 87.

34 Wood, *New England's Prospect*, p. 114.

35 Woodes Rogers, *A Cruising Voyage Round the World . . . Begun in 1708, and Finish'd in 1711* (London, 1712), pp. 124–5.

36 John Howell, *The Life and Adventures of Andrew Selkirk* (Edinburgh,

1829), pp. 72, 131–2.

37 George Anson, *A Voyage Round the World in the Years 1740, 41, 42, 43, 44* (London, 1853), p. 39.

38 Frederick Walpole, *Four Years in the Pacific in Her Majesty's Ship 'Collingwood' from 1844 to 1848*, 2nd edn (London, 1850), vol. I, pp. 374–6. See also T. H. Tizard et al., *Narrative of the Cruise of HMS Challenger*, pt 2 of *Report on the Scientific Results, 1873–76* (London, 1965), vol. I, p. 830.

39 Joseph Banks, *The Endeavour Journal of Joseph Banks 1768–1771*, ed. J. C. Beaglehole (London, 1963), vol. II, p. 7.

40 Thor Heyerdahl, *Aku-Aku* (New York, 1958), p. 278.

41 Boeck, 'The Norwegian Lobster-Fishery and Its History', p. 233.

42 Ibid.

43 Ibid., p. 237; see also Pontoppidan, *Natural History of Norway*, pp. 173–4.

44 Boeck, 'The Norwegian Lobster-Fishery and Its History', pp. 243–56.

45 M. Schele de Vere, *Wonders of the Deep* (New York, 1869), p. 196.

46 Coull, 'Shellfishing', p. 379.

47 Ibid., pp. 379–80.

48 Herrick, *Natural History of the American Lobster*, p. 174.

49 Ian Murray, personal communication, 23 October 2009.

4 BUILDING A BETTER LOBSTER TRAP

1 Henry David Thoreau, *Cape Cod* (London, 1987), p. 304.

2 Andres von Brandt, *Fish Catching Methods of the World*, 3rd edn (Farnham, Surrey, 1984), pp. 17, 151–2, 170–88, 328, 369.

3 Euell Gibbons, *Stalking the Blue-Eyed Scallop* (New York, 1972), pp. 300–2.

4 A. Castillo and H. A. Lessios, 'Lobster Fishery by the Kuna Indians in the San Blas Region of Panama (Kuna Yala)', *Crustaceana*, LXXIV/5 (May 2001), pp. 460–61, 472.

5 A. Hearn, V. Toral-Granda, C. Martinez and G. Reck, 'Biology and Fishery of the Galápagos Slipper Lobster', in *The Biology and*

Fisheries of the Slipper Lobster, ed. Kari L. Lavalli and Ehud Spanier (London, 2007), pp. 288–9, 302.

6 Bruce F. Phillips and Roy Melville-Smith, '*Panulirus* Species', in *Lobsters: Biology, Management, Aquaculture and Fisheries*, ed. Bruce F. Phillips (Oxford, 2006), p. 366; L. B. Holthuis, *FAO Species Catalogue: Volume 13, Marine Lobsters of the World: An Annotated and Illustrated Catalogue of Species of Interest to Fisheries Known to Date* (Rome, 1991), p. 149.

7 James R. Coull, 'Shellfishing', in *Scottish Life and Society: Boats, Fishing and the Sea*, ed. James R. Coull, Alexander Fenton and Kenneth Veitch (Edinburgh, 2008), vol. IV, p. 379; Richard Rathbun, 'The Lobster Fishery', in *The Fisheries and Fishery Industries of the United States*, section 5, ed. George Brown Goode *et al.* (Washington, DC, 1887), vol. II, p. 665.

8 Axel Boeck, 'The Norwegian Lobster-Fishery and Its History', in *United States Commission of Fish and Fisheries, Report of the Commissioner for 1873–4 and 1874–5*, pt III (Washington, DC, 1876), pp. 228–9.

9 Alan Spence, *Crab and Lobster Fishing* (Farnham, Surrey, 1989), p. 73.

10 John Whittaker, personal communication, 12 October 2009, Noank, Connecticut.

11 Fred Calabretta, 'Oral History Interview: Vivian Volovar' (Mystic Seaport Museum, Connecticut, 27 October 1993), typed transcript.

12 Personal communication from aboard *ssv Corwith Cramer* by VHF radio, 3 September 2008.

13 Johan C. Groeneveld, Raquel Goñi and Daniel Latrouite, '*Palinurus* Species', in *Lobsters: Biology, Management, Aquaculture and Fisheries*, ed. Bruce F. Phillips (Oxford, 2006), p. 397.

14 Phillips and Melville-Smith, '*Panulirus* Species', p. 372; Edakkepravan V. Radhakrishnan, Mary K. Manisseri and Vinay D. Deshmukh, 'Biology and Fishery of the Slipper Lobster, *Thenus orientalis*, in India', in *The Biology and Fisheries of the Slipper Lobster*, ed. Kari L. Lavalli and Ehud Spanier (London, 2007), pp. 309–10, 320–21.

15 Hearn, Toral-Granda, Martinez and Reck, 'Biology and Fishery of the Galápagos Slipper Lobster', p. 287.

16 Groeneveld, Goñi and Latrouite, '*Palinurus* Species', p. 400.

17 Analia Murias, 'Satellites Fixed on Lobster Fishing', *Fish Information and Services* (29 April 2010), available at http://fis.com, accessed 24 August 2010.

18 Staff and wire reports, 'Regulators Weigh Five-Year Ban in Southern NE: Fishermen are Opposed Despite Dwindling Stocks', *The Day* (New London, CT, 11 June 2010), p. A1.

19 John D. Booth, '*Jasus* Species', in *Lobsters: Biology, Management, Aquaculture and Fisheries*, ed. Bruce F. Phillips (Oxford, 2006), pp. 349–50; Phillips and Melville-Smith, '*Panulirus* Species', p. 359; J. Stanley Cobb and Kathleen M. Castro, '*Homarus* species', in *Lobsters: Biology, Management, Aquaculture and Fisheries*, ed. Bruce F. Phillips (Oxford, 2006), p. 327; Atlantic States Marine Fisheries Commission, 'Press Release: American Lobster Stock Assessment Yields Mixed Results' (7 May 2009), pp. 1–2.

20 Nadia Dewhurst, 'Assessing the Status of All the World's Lobster Species', *Lobster Newsletter*, XXIII/1 (April 2010), pp. 5–6.

21 Ibid., p. 6.

22 Gardner Pinfold Consulting Economists Ltd for Agriculture and Agri-Food Canada, 'Benchmarking Study on Canadian Lobster' (March 2006), p. i.

23 The Lobster Institute, 'Estimated Economic Impact of the Lobster Industry' (Orono, ME, 2004), brochure.

24 John N. Cobb, 'The Lobster Fishery in Maine', *Bulletin of the United States Fish Commission* (Washington, DC, 1900), p. 243.

25 Kenneth R. Martin and Nathan R. Lipfert, *Lobstering and the Maine Coast* (Bath, ME, 1985), p. 33.

26 Ibid., pp. 33–5.

27 Ibid.

28 Moses Henry Perley, *Reports on the Sea and River Fisheries of New Brunswick*, 2nd edn (Fredericton, NB, 1852), p. 20.

29 John J. Rowan, *The Emigrant and Sportsman in Canada* (Montreal, 1881), p. 138.

30 Farley Mowat, *Sea of Slaughter* (London, 1986), p. 200.

31 Rowan, *The Emigrant and Sportsman in Canada*, p. 137.

32 Mowat, *Sea of Slaughter*, p. 201.

33 W. H. Bishop, *The Lobster at Home in Maine Waters* (unspecified, 1881), p. 9.

34 Frank Nicosia and Kari Lavalli, 'Homarid Lobster Hatcheries: Their History and Role in Research, Management, and Aquaculture', *Marine Fisheries Review*, LXI/2 (1999), p. 6.

35 Rathbun, 'The Lobster Fishery', pp. 659, 696–7; W. F. Witcher, Commissioner of Fisheries, Department of Marine and Fisheries, *Annual Report for 1873*, in Joseph Gough, *Managing Canada's Fisheries: From Early Days to the Year 2000* (Georgetown, ON, 2006), pp. 123–4.

36 Alfred Goldsborough Mayer, *Sea-shore Life: The Invertebrates of the New York Coast* (New York, 1905), p. 84.

37 Holman F. Day, 'Good-by Lobster', *Up in Maine: Stories of Yankee Life Told in Verse* (Boston, 1904), pp. 110–11.

38 Francis Hobart Herrick, *Address of Francis H. Herrick, Ph.D., Sc.D.: The Failure of the Lobster Fisheries and How to Save Them from Commercial Extinction* (Augusta, ME, 1915), p. 14 (as in Martin and Lipfert, *Lobstering and the Maine Coast*, p. 55).

39 Philip Conkling and Anne Hayden, *Lobsters Great and Small: How Scientists and Fishermen are Changing our Understanding of a Maine Icon* (Rockland, ME, 2002), p. 8.

40 Anne Hayden, personal communication, 5 August 2009.

41 Anne Hayden, personal communication, 19 August 2009, Brunswick, Maine; Conkling and Hayden, *Lobsters Great and Small*, pp. 8–11.

42 Luis Marden, 'The American Lobster, Delectable Cannibal', *National Geographic*, CXLIII/4 (April 1973), p. 463.

43 Scott Allen, 'Biologists say Lobster Level in a Pinch', *Boston Globe* (24 July 1998), p. A1.

44 Monterey Bay Aquarium Foundation, 'Seafood Watch: Northeast Sustainable Seafood Guide' (Monterey, CA, July 2010), available at www.montereybayaquarium.org, accessed 24 August 2010.

45 Alexandre Dumas, *Dictionary of Cuisine*, trans. and ed. Louis Colman (London, 1990), pp. 162–3.

46 Anonymous fishmonger, personal communication, 28 February 2010, Seattle, Washington.

5 TO BOIL OR NOT TO BOIL

1 Alexandre Dumas, *Dictionary of Cuisine*, trans. and ed. Louis Colman (London, 1990), p. 160.

2 Philip Conkling and Anne Hayden, *Lobsters Great and Small: How Scientists and Fishermen are Changing our Understanding of a Maine Icon* (Rockland, ME, 2002), pp. 3–5.

3 Kelly Woods, Director and Chair of the Advertising/Public Relations Committee, Maine Lobster Festival, personal communication, 26 January 2010.

4 International Federation of Competitive Eating/Major League Eating, 'Records' (January 2011), available at www.ifoce.com, accessed 3 January 2011.

5 Katie Zezima, 'Lobsters Race, Slowly, In Bar Harbor', *The New York Times* (5 July 2009), p. A16.

6 William Bradford, *History of Plymouth Plantation*, ed. Charles Deane (Boston, 1856), p. 146.

7 William Wood, *New England's Prospect*, ed. Alden T. Vaughan (Amherst, MA, 1993), p. 56.

8 Sandy Oliver, 'The Truth about Spices, Lobsters, and Flaming Ladies', *The Debunk-House, Food History News* (May 2008), available at www.foodhistorynews.com, accessed 24 August 2010.

9 Sandy Oliver, personal communication, 9 November 2009.

10 Sandra L. Oliver, *Saltwater Foodways* (Mystic, CT, 1995), p. 382.

11 Richard Rathbun, 'The Lobster Fishery', in *The Fisheries and Fishery Industries of the United States*, section 5, ed. George Brown Goode et al. (Washington, DC, 1887), vol. II, p. 659.

12 'The Rich Red Lobster: How He is Caught and Brought to Market', *New York Times* (9 April 1882), p. 4.

13 George H. Lewis, 'The Maine Lobster as Regional Icon:

Competing Images over Time and Social Class', in *The Taste of American Place: A Reader on Regional and Ethnic Foods*, ed. Barbara G. Shortridge and James R. Shortridge (Oxford, 1998), p. 71.

14 Robert Blakey, *Old Faces in New Masks* (London, 1859), p. 360.

15 Maguelonne Touissaint-Samat, *A History of Food*, trans. Anthea Bell (Oxford, 1994), p. 387; W. B. Lord, *Crab, Shrimp & Lobster Lore* (London, 1867), p. 103.

16 John Edwards, *The Roman Cookery of Apicius* (Washington, DC, 1984), p. 240.

17 Brian Fagan, *Fish on Friday: Feasting, Fasting, and the Discovery of the New World* (New York, 2006), p. 36; Terence Scully, *The Art of Cookery in the Middle Ages* (Woodbridge, Suffolk, 1995), p. 33.

18 Terence Scully, ed., *The Viandier of Taillevent: An Edition of All Extant Manuscripts* (Ottawa, 1988), p. 243.

19 Scully, *The Art of Cookery in the Middle Ages*, p. 90.

20 C. Anne Wilson, *Food and Drink in Britain: From the Stone Age to the 19th Century* (Chicago, 2003), pp. 47, 49.

21 Robert May, *The Accomplisht Cook, or the Art and Mystery of Cookery*, 4th edn (London, 1678), p. 403.

22 Alexander Pope, 'A Farewell to London in the Year 1715', *The Major Works*, ed. Pat Rogers (Oxford, 2006), p. 119.

23 Hannah Glasse, *The Art of Cookery Made Plain and Easy* (Alexandria, VA, 1805), ed. Karen Hess (Bedford, MA, 1997), p. 13.

24 E. Smith, *The Compleat Housewife: or, Accomplish'd Gentlewoman's Companion*, facs. of 15th edn (1753) and 18th edn (1773) (London, 1968), p. 55.

25 Ibid., p. 54.

26 Charles Dickens, *The Personal History of David Copperfield*, ed. Trevor Blount (London, 1986), pp. 80, 156, 545, 920.

27 'Cookery: Dishes for a Supper-Party', *Household Words*, II/36, ed. Charles Dickens (31 December 1881), p. 195.

28 'Cookery: Dishes of Fish', *Household Words*, II/48, ed. Charles Dickens (25 March 1882), p. 438.

29 Susan M. Rossi-Wilcox, *Dinner for Dickens: The Culinary History of Mrs Charles Dickens's Menu Books Including a Transcript of* What

Shall We Have for Dinner *by 'Lady Maria Clutterbuck'* (Blackawton, Totnes, 2005), p. 60.

30 Eliza Acton, *Modern Cookery For Private Families, Reduced to a System of Easy Practice*, new and enlarged edn (London, 1868); Mrs D. A. Lincoln, *Mrs Lincoln's Boston Cooking School Cook Book* [*Mrs Lincoln's Boston Cook Book*] [1884 text] (Mineola, NY, 1996).

31 Glen A. Jones, '"Quite the Choicest Protein Dish": The Costs of Consuming Seafood in American Restaurants, 1850–2006', in *Oceans Past: Management Insights from the History of Marine Animal Populations*, ed. David J. Starkey, Paul Holm and Michaela Barnard (London, 2008), p. 52, fig. 4.3.

32 Ibid., p. 73.

33 Kevin Jordan, writer and director, *Brooklyn Lobster*, Meadowbrook Pictures (2005).

34 Blakey, *Old Faces in New Masks*, p. 361.

35 Tobias Venner, *Via Recta ad Vitam Longam, or A Plaine Philosophical Discourse of the Nature, faculties, and effects of all such things . . .* (London, 1620), p. 82.

36 Ken Albala, *Eating Right in the Renaissance* (London, 2002), p. 150.

37 John Smith, 'A Rhapsody upon a Lobster, POEM Burlesque', *Poems upon Several Occasions* (1713), p. 184, available at lion.chadwyck.com, accessed 24 August 2010.

38 John Gay, 'To a Young Lady, with some lampreys', *The Poetical Works of John Gay*, ed. Dr. Johnson (Boston, 1854), vol. II, p. 118.

39 Jasper White, *Lobster at Home* (New York, 1998), p. 27.

40 James Soderholm, *Fantasy, Forgery, and the Byron Legend* (Lexington, KY, 1996), p. 104. Byron's emphasis.

41 Lewis A. Erenberg, *Steppin' Out: New York Nightlife and the Transformation of American Culture 1890–1930* (London, 1984), p. 40.

42 G. Legman, 'Documentation for "Wolf" and "Lobster"', *American Speech*, XXIV/2 (April 1949), p. 155.

43 Andrew Fisher, personal communication, 30 October 2009, Santa Cruz, California.

44 Ron Howard, director, written by Lowell Ganz, Babaloo Mandel and Bruce Jay Friedman, *Splash*, Touchstone Pictures (1984).

45 Shirley Jump, *The Angel Craved Lobster* (New York, 2005), p. 353.
46 Poppy Cannon and Patricia Brooks, *The Presidents' Cookbook: Practical Recipes from George Washington to the Present* (New York, 1968), p. 415. See also the opening scene of the slapstick film *The Naked Gun 2 1/2* (1991).
47 White, *Lobster at Home*, p. 2; Helen Siegel and Karen Gillingham, *The Totally Lobster Cookbook* (Berkeley, CA, 1997), p. 39.
48 Platina, *On Right Pleasure and Good Health*, trans. and ed. Mary Ella Milham (Tempe, AZ, 1998), p. 431.
49 Edouard de Pomiane, *Cooking with Pomiane*, trans. and ed. Peggie Benton (New York, 2001), p. 78.
50 David Foster Wallace, 'Consider the Lobster', *Gourmet* (August 2004), p. 64.
51 Woody Allen, director, co-written with Marshall Brickman, *Annie Hall*, United Artists (1977).
52 Kim Severson, 'Film Food, Ready for Its "Bon Appetit"', *New York Times* (29 July 2009), p. D1.
53 For example: Walter Beverley Crane, Letter to the Editor: 'A Plea for the Lobster', *New York Times*, 18 June 1907; Edith Carrington, 'Crabs and Lobsters', *The Animals' Friend*, II (London, 1895–6), pp. 209–11.
54 Elizabeth Murray, 'Observations on Methods of Killing Lobsters', *Annual Report, Marine Biological Station Port Erin, 1961*, no. 74 (Liverpool, 1962), p. 33.
55 Ibid., pp. 41–2.
56 Wallace, 'Consider the Lobster', p. 64.

6 LOBSTER TALES

1 Rachel Carson 'Undersea', *Lost Woods: The Discovered Writing of Rachel Carson*, ed. Linda Lear (Boston, 1998), p. 7.
2 My retelling of 'Pu-nia' here is adapted from Padraic Colum's version, recorded from his travels in Hawaii and published in *Tales and Legends of Hawaii: At the Gateways of the Day* (New Haven, CT, 1924), vol. I, pp. 1–6. I have directly incorporated some

of Colum's dialogue for Pu-nia.

3 Ibid., p. 6.
4 Lee Wardlaw, *Punia and the King of Sharks*, illus. Felipe Dávalos (New York, 1997), p. 2.
5 Henry A. Wise ('Harry Gringo'), *Tales for the Marines* (Boston, 1857), pp. 23–4.
6 Robert Blakey, *Old Faces in New Masks* (London, 1859), p. 372.
7 Charles Kingsley, *The Water-Babies: A Fairy Tale for a Land-Baby*, new edn (London, 1889), pp. 142–4.
8 Ibid., pp. 176–81.
9 Anne Sexton, 'Lobster', *45 Mercy Street* (Boston, 1976), p. 34.
10 George Mackay Brown, *For the Islands I Sing: An Autobiography* (London, 1997), p. 27.
11 George Mackay Brown, 'Lobster' [1986], in *The Oxford Book of Creatures*, ed. Fleur Adcock and Jacqueline Simms (Oxford, 1995), p. 113.
12 'Lobster', *Oxford English Dictionary*, 2nd edn (Oxford, 1989).
13 Walt Whitman, 'A Song of Joys', *Leaves of Grass and Other Writings*, ed. Michael Moon (London, 2002), p. 151.
14 Leo Walmsley, *Phantom Lobster* (London, 1948), p. 46.
15 Leo Walmsley, *Three Fevers* (London, 1947), pp. 29, 69, 90.
16 Ibid., p. 92.
17 Louise Dickinson Rich, *The Peninsula* (New York, 1958), pp. 54–5.
18 Ibid., pp. 96, 98.
19 Ibid., p. 87.
20 George H. Lewis, 'The Maine Lobster as Regional Icon: Competing Images over Time and Social Class', in *The Taste of American Place: A Reader on Regional and Ethnic Foods*, ed. Barbara G. Shortridge and James R. Shortridge (Oxford, 1998), p. 74.
21 E. B. White (co-writer, narrator) and Arthur Zegart (co-writer, director), *A Maine Lobsterman, or A Day in the Life of a Fisherman*, 'Omnibus'/CBS (New York, 1954).
22 Ibid.
23 Arthur Train, 'The Viking's Daughter', *When Tutt Meets Tutt* (New York, 1927), p. 112.

24 Rich, *The Peninsula*, p. 268.

25 Linda Greenlaw, *The Lobster Chronicles: Life on a Very Small Island* (New York, 2002), p. 116.

26 Ibid., p. 145.

27 Ibid., p. 5.

28 Tim Winton, *Dirt Music* (London, 2001), p. 304.

29 Elizabeth Gilbert, *Stern Men* (Boston, 2000), pp. 144–5.

30 Ibid., p. 236.

31 Ibid., p. 5.

32 Jack London, 'The Water Baby', *The Complete Short Stories of Jack London*, ed. E. Labor, R. C. Leitz, III and I. M. Shepard (Stanford, CA, 1993), vol. III, p. 2490.

33 Ibid., p. 2492.

34 Ibid., p. 2493.

35 Earle Labor, 'Jack London's Pacific World', in *Critical Essays on Jack London*, ed. Jacqueline Tavernier-Courbin (Boston, 1983), pp. 217–19.

36 James I. McClintock, *White Logic: Jack London's Short Stories [Jack London's Strong Truths]* (Grand Rapids, MI, 1975), p. 163.

37 Calvin Tomkins, 'The Turnaround Artist', *New Yorker*, 23 April 2007, p. 60.

38 Laurent Le Bon, 'Interview with Jeff Koons', *Jeff Koons Versailles* (Paris, 2008), p. 111.

39 Guillaume Lecasble, *Lobster*, trans. Polly McLean (Sawtry, Cambs, 2005), p. 26.

40 For example: Hannah Flagg Gould, 'The Envious Lobster', *Poems* (Boston, 1841), vol. III, pp. 100–101; John Godfrey Saxe, 'The Force of Example: A Fable', *The Poetical Works of John Godfrey Saxe* (Boston, 1889), p. 216.

41 Lewis Carroll, *The Annotated Alice: Alice's Adventures in Wonderland & Through the Looking Glass*, ed. Martin Gardner (New York, 1960), p. 139.

42 Ibid.

43 Théophile Gautier, *My Fantoms*, trans. Richard Holmes (London, 1976), pp. 149–50.

44 Scott Horton, 'Nerval: A Man and His Lobster', *Harper's* (12 October 2008).

45 William Golding, *Pincher Martin* (also *The Two Deaths of Christopher Martin*) (New York, 1956), p. 116.

46 Samuel Beckett, 'Dante and the Lobster', *Samuel Beckett: The Grove Centenary Edition: Poems, Short Fiction, Criticism*, ed. Paul Auster (New York, 2006), vol. IV, p. 87.

47 Ibid., p. 88.

48 Jean-Louis Chevalier, interview with 'A. S. Byatt – b. 1936', *Journal of the Short Story in English* [Online], 41 (Autumn 2003), p. 7, available at jsse.revues.org/index323.html, accessed 24 August 2010.

49 A. S. Byatt, 'The Chinese Lobster', *The Matisse Stories* (London, 1993), p. 134.

50 Ibid.

7 FEELERS

1 George H. Lewis, 'The Maine Lobster as Regional Icon: Competing Images over Time and Social Class', *The Taste of American Place: A Reader on Regional and Ethnic Foods*, ed. Barbara G. Shortridge and James R. Shortridge (Oxford, 1998), p. 80.

2 Puerto Nuevo Lobster, 'Home' (2010), available at www.puerto-nuevolobster.com, accessed 24 August 2010; Andrea Sachs, 'Mexico's Little Lobster Town', *Washington Post* (9 June 2002).

3 Tom Powers, personal communication, 11 March 2009.

4 Bennet M. Allen, 'Notes on the Spiny Lobster (*Panulirus interruptus*) of the California Coast', *University of California Publications in Zoology*, XVI/12 (17 March 1916), p. 139.

5 Kevin Lewand, personal communication, 30 July 2009, Monterey, California.

6 Jules Verne, *The Complete Twenty Thousand Leagues under the Sea* [1871 edn], ed. and trans. Emanuel J. Mickel (Bloomington, IN, 1991), p. 370.

7 Francis Hobart Herrick, *Natural History of the American Lobster* (Washington, DC, 1911), p. 194.

8   J. S. Cobb and K. M. Castro, '*Homarus* Species', in *Lobsters: Biology, Management, Aquaculture and Fisheries*, ed. Bruce F. Phillips (Oxford, 2006), pp. 314–15.

9   Nelson M. Ehrhardt, 'Estimating Growth of the Florida Spiny Lobster, *Panulirus argus*, From Molt Frequency and Size Increment Data from Tag and Recapture Experiments', *Fisheries Research*, XCIII/3 (September 2008), pp. 332–7; Kristine C. Barsky, 'California Spiny Lobster', in *California's Living Marine Resources: A Status Report* (2001), p. 100.

10 *Thaumastochelopsis brucei* and *wardi*; Shane T. Ahyong, Ka-Hou Chu and Tin-Yam Chan, 'Description of a New Species of *Thaumastochelopsis* from the Coral Sea', *Bulletin of Marine Science*, LXXX/1 (2007), p. 201.

11 Tin-Yam Chan, 'Annotatated Checklist of the World's Marine Lobsters', *The Raffles Bulletin of Zoology*, supplement no. 23 (31 October 2010), pp. 153–4.

12 Bruce F. Phillips and Roy Melville-Smith, '*Panulirus* Species', in *Lobsters: Biology, Management, Aquaculture and Fisheries*, ed. Bruce F. Phillips (Oxford, 2006), p. 376; M. Vijaykumaran, 'Conference Synthesis: Recent Advances in Lobster Biology, Aquaculture and Management (RALBAM 2010, Chennai, India, January 2010', *Lobster Newsletter*, XXIII/1 (April 2010), p. 4; Frank Nicosia and Kari Lavalli, 'Homarid Lobster Hatcheries: Their History and Role in Research, Management, and Aquaculture', *Marine Fisheries Review*, LXI/2 (1999), pp. 1–57.

13 Bruce F. Phillips, 'Conclusions', in *Lobsters: Biology, Management, Aquaculture and Fisheries*, ed. Bruce F. Phillips (Oxford, 2006), p. 498.

14 Blue Zoo Aquatics, 'Lobster', available at www.bluezooaquatics.com, accessed 24 August 2010; Ret Talbot, personal communication, 11 November 2009, Laguna Beach, CA; Stanley Cobb, personal communication, 14 November 2009, Kingston, RI.

15 Henry Liascos, personal communication, 11 October and 27 December 2009.

16 Elizabeth S. Pritchard, ed., *Fisheries of the United States 2008*
    (Silver Spring, MD, 2009), p. 59.
17 'Eastern Canada Offshore Lobster Fishery gains MSC
    Certification', *Marine Stewardship Council* (2 June 2010), available
    at www.msc.org, accessed 3 January 2011.
18 'Track a Fishery: Normandy and Jersey Lobster', *Marine
    Stewardship Council* (19 August 2010), available at www.msc.org,
    accessed 3 January 2011.
19 Callum Roberts, *The Unnatural History of the Sea* (London, 2007),
    p. 319.
20 Ibid., pp. 330–31.
21 Ian Murray, personal communication, 23 October 2009.
22 S. H. Jury, H. Howell, D. F. O'Grady and W. H. Watson, III,
    'Lobster Trap Video: *In Situ* Video Surveillance of the Behaviour
    of *Homarus americanus* in and around Traps', *Marine and
    Freshwater Research*, LII (2001), pp. 1125–32. Similar studies are
    being conducted in other countries such as Australia.
23 Lisa Mossey, Ocean Choice International, personal communica-
    tion, 16 August 2010.
24 Shucks Maine Lobster, 'Products' (2009), available at
    www.shucksmaine.com, accessed 24 August 2010.
25 Crustastun, 'Products: The Crustastun: World's First Humane
    Electronic Crustacean Stunner' (2009), available at www.crustas-
    tun.com, accessed 24 August 2010.
26 Mitchell Rosen, personal communication, 27 August 2009, New
    York.

Bibliography

Acheson, James M., *Capturing the Commons: Devising Institutions to Manage the Maine Lobster Industry* (Hanover, NH, 2003)

Chan, Tin-Yam, 'Annotated Checklist of the World's Marine Lobsters', *The Raffles Bulletin of Zoology*, supplement no. 23 (31 October 2010), pp. 153–81.

Corson, Trevor, *The Secret Life of Lobsters: How Fishermen and Scientists Are Unraveling the Mysteries of Our Favorite Crustacean* (New York, 2004)

Gilbert, Elizabeth, *Stern Men* (Boston, 2000)

Greenlaw, Linda, *The Lobster Chronicles: Life on a Very Small Island* (New York, 2002)

Herrick, Francis Hobart, *Natural History of the American Lobster* (Washington, DC, 1911)

Holthuis, L. B., *FAO Species Catalogue: Volume 13, Marine Lobsters of the World: An Annotated and Illustrated Catalogue of Species of Interest to Fisheries Known to Date* (Rome, 1991)

Martin, Kenneth R. and Nathan R. Lipfert, *Lobstering and the Maine Coast* (Bath, ME, 1985)

Melville-Smith, Roy, and Richard A. Wahle, eds, 'The Lobster Newsletter' (North Beach, WA, Australia and Walpole, ME, USA, published annually or biannually), available at www.fish.wa.gov.au/the_lobster_newsletter/Index.html

Phillips, Bruce F., ed., *Lobsters: Biology, Management, Aquaculture and Fisheries* (Oxford, 2006)

Rathbun, Richard, 'The Lobster Fishery', in *The Fisheries and Fishery*

Industries of the United States, section 5, vol. II, ed. George Brown
    Goode et al. (Washington, DC, 1887)
Spence, Alan, *Crab and Lobster Fishing* (Farnham, Surrey, 1989)
Wallace, David Foster, 'Consider the Lobster', *Gourmet* (August 2004)
Walmsley, Leo, *Three Fevers* (London, 1932)
—, *Phantom Lobster* (London, 1933)
Wardlaw, Lee, *Punia and the King of Sharks*, illus. Felipe Dávalos
    (New York, 1997)
White, Jasper, *Lobster at Home* (New York, 1998)

Associations and Websites

ATLANTIC CANADA LOBSTER
Atlantic Canada Lobster and Seafood Promotion Group
www.tastelobster.ca

FISH WATCH: U.S. SEAFOOD FACTS
National Marine Fisheries Service
1315 East West Highway
Silver Spring, MD 20910 USA
www.nmfs.noaa.gov/fishwatch

FISHERIES AND OCEANS CANADA (DFO)
Maritimes Region
PO Box 1035
Dartmouth NS B2Y 4T3 Canada
www.dfo-mpo.gc.ca

THE FOOD TIMELINE
Lynne Olver, editor and researcher
www.foodtimeline.org

THE LOBSTER INSTITUTE
210 Rogers Hall
The University of Maine
Orono, ME 04469 USA
www.lobsterinstitute.org

PEOPLE FOR THE ETHICAL TREATMENT OF ANIMALS
501 Front Street
Norfolk, VA 23510 USA
www.peta.org

MAINE MARITIME MUSEUM
243 Washington Street
Bath, ME 04530 USA
www.mainemaritimemuseum.org

MARINE LOBSTERS OF THE WORLD
L. B. Holthuis
World Biodiversity Database
http://nlbif.eti.uva.nl/bis/lobsters.php

MARINE STEWARDSHIP COUNCIL
(Head Office)
6–20 Elizabeth Street
London SW1W 9RB UK
www.msc.org

SCOTTISH FISHERIES MUSEUM
St Ayles, Harbourhead
Anstruther, Fife
UK, KY10 3AB
www.scotfishmuseum.org

SEAFOOD WATCH
Monterey Bay Aquarium Foundation
886 Cannery Row
Monterey, CA 93940 USA
www.montereybayaquarium.org/cr/seafoodwatch.aspx

SEARCHABLE SEA LITERATURE
The Maritime Studies Program of
Williams College and Mystic Seaport
75 Greenmanville Avenue
Mystic, CT 06355 USA
www.williams.edu/williamsmystic/SeaLitSearchable/SeaLitSearchab
le.html

SHELLFISH ASSOCIATION OF GREAT BRITAIN
Fishmongers' Hall
London Bridge, London EC4R 9EL UK
www.shellfish.org.uk

THE WALMSLEY SOCIETY
April Cottage
1 Brand Road
Hampden Park, Eastbourne BN22 9PX UK
www.walmsleysoc.org

WESTERN ROCK LOBSTER COUNCIL
PO Box 1605
Frermantle, WE 6959 AU
www.rocklobsterwa.com

Acknowledgements

Captain John Whittaker aboard *Whistler* was a patient and knowledgeable boss and later equally so in helping with this project. The Maritime Studies Program of Williams College and Mystic Seaport provided full logistical support. The librarians at Mystic Seaport, Kemble House Basement, University of California Santa Cruz, Moss Landing Marine Laboratories, NOAA Southeast Fisheries Science Center, Williams College and Connecticut College were abundantly helpful and brilliant. Kresge College at UCSC and The Moss Landing Marine Laboratories provided research space and opportunities. 'Lobster' is reprinted in full on p. 136 by kind permission of the executors of George Mackay Brown's estate.

Several individuals not mentioned within the text deserve special thanks: James Carlton, Vicki Sheng, Susan Wishon, Robert Prescott, Jen Gordon, Nathan Lipfert, the film crew of 'Catch It!', Jennifer Finn, Susan Beegel, Kari Lavalli, Douglas Pezzack, Susan Schnur, Sue Vickers Tordoff and Fred Lane. Stanley Cobb, Daniel Brayton and Rebecca Kessler generously offered their time as skilled outside readers. As editors Jonathan Burt, Martha Jay and Michael Leaman helped improve the text immensely. Harry Gilonis did the same for the images.

Thank you to my tolerant wife and smart colleague Lisa Gilbert as well as newborn Alice Day. The book is dedicated to my brother David.

Photo Acknowledgements

The author and publishers wish to express their thanks to the below sources of illustrative material and/or permission to reproduce it.

From Eliza Acton, *Modern Cookery for Private Families...* (London, 1868): pp. 112, 113; American Museum of Natural History, New York: p. 78; collection of the author: p. 92; photo courtesy of the author: p. 47; Bibliothèque Centrale du Museum National d'Histoire Naturelle, Paris: p. 52; from W. H. Bishop, *The Lobster at Home in Maine Waters* (n.p., 1881): pp. 83, 94; from Robert Blakey, *Old Faces in New Masks* (London, 1859): p. 60; Courtesy Boothbay Region Historical Society, Boothbay Harbor, Maine: p. 114; British Library, London (All Rights Reserved, © The British Library Board): p. 68; photo courtesy of the John Carter Brown Library at Brown University, Providence, Rhode Island: p. 56; Canada Science and Technology Museum, Ottawa: p. 100; from Lewis Carroll, *Alice's Adventures in Wonderland* (London, 1865): p. 155; reproduced courtesy of the artist (Malcolm Cheape): p. 23; courtesy of the Art History Department (Caroline Black Print Collection), Connecticut College, New London, Connecticut: p. 14 (foot); photo courtesy Crustastun: p. 174; © Salvador Dalí, Fundació Gala-Salvador Dalí / Artists Rights Society (ARS), New York 2011: p. 149; Peter de Sève, *The New Yorker*, Condé Nast Archive, © Condé Nast: p. 20; photo Charles Derby (first published in *Journal of Crustacean Biology*, 1982): p. 28; Farnsworth Art Museum (gift of James Moore), and by permission of Black Star: p. 8; photo Robert Fenner (WetWebMedia): p. 34; photo James W. Fetzner, Jr, Carnegie Museum of Natural History, Pittsburgh, Pennsylvania: p. 55; The Fishmongers' Company, London: p. 72; photos © David Fleetham (www.davidfleetham.com): pp. 26, 168; William B. Folsom, National Oceanic and Atmospheric Administration/Department of Commerce (Photo Library): pp. 85, 161; courtesy Food and Agriculture Organization of the United Nations: p. 18; *Frank Leslie's Popular Monthly*, vol. 7, no. 2 (February 1879): p. 138; photo George French, courtesy Maine State Archives Collection, Augusta, Maine: p. 9; photo Brian Gauvin: p. 40; Lisa Gilbert (2010) [see also fig. 4 from F. W. Nicosia and K. L. Lavalli, 'Homarid lobster hatcheries: Their history and role in research, management, and aquaculture', in *Maritime Fisheries Review*, vol. 61, no. 2 (1999)]: p. 91; © Goro Uno, Haga Library, Tokyo: p. 106; from Ernst Haeckel, *Kunstformen der Natur* (Leipzig & Vienna, 1904): p. 48; photo courtesy Hamilton College Library, Clinton, New York: p. 138; Harvard University Mercator Globes collection, Pusey Library, Harvard College Library, Cambridge, Massachusetts: p. 51; from Francis Hobart Herrick, 'The American Lobster: a Study of its Habits and Development', in the *Bulletin of the United States Fish Commission*, vol. 15 (1895): p. 46; from Francis Hobart Herrick, *Natural History of the American Lobster* (Washington, DC, 1911): pp. 36, 43; photo Jim Higgins: p. 27; from L. B. Holthuis, *UN Food and Agriculture Organization Species Catalogue Vol. 13 Marine Lobsters of the World: An Annotated and Illustrated Catalogue of Species of Interest to Fisheries Known to Date* (Rome, 1991): p. 18; Images Canada: p. 100; Instituto Nacional de Cultura e Historia, Belize: p. 57; from Dahlov Ipcar, *Lobsterman* (Camden, Maine: Down East Books, 1978); © 1962 by Dahlov Ipcar; reproduced courtesy Isle au Haut Historical Society: p. 93; photo courtesy Greg James: p. 169; from John Jonston, *Historiae Naturalis de Quadrupedibus libri. Cum aeneis figuris...* (Amsterdam, 1657): p. 14 (top); photo Paul Kay/Splashdown Direct/Rex Features: p. 175; from Charles Kingsley, *The Water-Babies, A Fairy Tale for a Land Baby* (New York, 1916), photo courtesy of the Library of Congress, Washington, DC: p. 133; © Jeff Koons: p. 150; from William Elford Leach, *Malacostraca Podophthalmata Britanniæ; or, Descriptions of such British Species of the Linnean Genus Cancer as have their Eyes Elevated on Footstalks. Illustrated with Figures [...] by James Sowerby...* (London, 1815): p. 53; Library of Congress, Washington, DC (Prints and Photographs Division): pp. 107, 119, 154; from Joseph Lycett, *Drawings of the Natives & Scenery of Van Diemens Land 1830*: p. 67; reprinted with permission of McIntosh & Otis, Inc: p. 121; from Olaus Magnus, *Historia de gentibus septentrionalibus* (Rome, 1555): p. 59; Collections of Maine Historical Society (Maine Memory Network, www.mainememory.net): pp. 143, 163; photo Maine State Aquarium & the Maine State Department of Marine Resources Education Division, Boothbay Harbor, Maine: p. 31; photo Iain Mathews, The Bell Pettigrew Museum of Natural History, St Andrews University, Scotland: p. 54; image © The Metropolitan Museum of Art/Art Resource, New York (© Estate George Platt Lynes): p. 152; photo Rosanna Milligan: p. 15; photo Fred G. Milliken: p. 163; © Mystic Seaport, Photography Collection, Mystic, Connecticut, www.mysticseaport.org: p. 111; courtesy Fotoarkivet, Nasjonalbiblioteket, Oslo: p. 71; National Library of Australia, Canberra: p. 67; National Maritime Museum, London: p. 141; photos courtesy The National Oceanic and Atmospheric Administration/United States Department of Commerce: pp. 45 (Photo Library), 63 (Northeast Fisheries Science Center); courtesy Ocean Choice International: p. 173; courtesy Oceanographic Research Institute Durban, South Africa: p. 86; photo Randy Olson, *National Geographic*: p. 79 (foot); photo Winfield Parks, *National Geographic*: p. 81; photo © Jorge Pérez de Lara: p. 57; © PETA

(People for the Ethical Treatment of Animals): p. 125; photo © PETA (People for the Ethical Treatment of Animals): p. 126; photo Tom Powers: p. 162; photo Norma Prause, *National Fisherman*, 22 June 2002: p. 145; private collections: pp. 23, 150; courtesy Redondo Beach Chamber of Commerce & Visitors Bureau: p. 150; from Louis Renard, *Poissons, Ecrevisses et Crabes de diverses Couleurs et Figures Extraordinaires, que l'on trouve autour des Isles Moluques, et sur les Côtes des Terres Australes . . . [Histoire Naturelle des plus rares Curiositez de la Mar des Indes]* (Amsterdam, 1754): p. 32; Revere Memorial Library, Isle au Haut, Maine: pp. 93, 96; Rijksmuseum, Amsterdam: p. 69; Bill Ronalds (courtesy Kelly Woods/Maine Lobster Festival: p. 100; from Polydore Roux, *Crustacés de la Méditerranée et de son Littoral...* (Paris, 1828): p. 40; from Walter Ryff, *Thierbuch Alberti Magni: Von Art Natur vnd Eygenschafft der Thierer, Als nemlich von Vierfüsigen, Vögeln, Fyschen, Schlangen oder kriechenden Thieren, Vnd vonden kleinen gewürmen die man Jnsecta nennet; Mit jhren Contrafactur Figuren . . .* (Frankfurt-am-Main, 1545): p. 58; photo Heikki Saukkomaa/Rex Features: p. 151; map by Susan Schnur, 2010 (data courtesy Food and Agriculture Organization of the United Nations): pp. 10–11; courtesy Scottish Fisheries Museum, Anstruther, Fife: pp. 73, 87; Staatliche Museen, Berlin: p. 137; photo James L. Stanfield, *National Geographic*: p. 79 (top); Tate, London (© Tate, London, 2008): p. 149; photo Tin-Yam Chan, National Taiwan Ocean University, Keelung: p. 166; photo John C. Turner, courtesy Stanley G. French: p. 96; University of St Andrews, Scotland: p. 74; Vispix: p. 165; from Leo Walmsley 'Between the Heather and the North Sea', *National Geographic*, vol. 63, No. 2 (Feb. 1933), reproduced by kind permission of Stephanie Walmsley: pp. 139, 140; from Lee Wardlaw, *Punia and the King of Sharks: A Hawaiian Folktale* (New York, 1997), illustrated by Felipe Dávalos-Gonzales, illustrations © 1997 by Felipe Dávalos-Gonzales, used by permission of Dial Books for Young Readers, a division of Penguin Young Readers Group – all rights reserved: p. 158; courtesy John Whittaker: p. 77; photo Randy Wilder, © Monterey Bay Aquarium, Monterey, California: p. 30; photo Anders Beer Wilse/Norsk Folkemuseum, Oslo: p. 71; photo photo Erik Zobrist, The National Oceanic and Atmospheric Administration/ United States Department of Commerce: p. 101; photos © Zoological Society of London: pp. 14 (top), 40, 53.

Index